A Light
IN DARK PLACES

A Light

IN DARK PLACES

A story of heartbreak, survival and redemption.

by
Jennifer Graves and Emily Clawson

ISBN-13:
978-1490426112

ISBN-10:
1490426116

Cover design by Steven Novak www.novakillustration.com
Cover photo by Amber Hardman www.hardmanphotography.com
Author photo by Tamra Hyde www.modernexpressionsphoto.com
Edited by Jenn Wilks

Printed in the United States of America

10 9 8 7 6 5 4 3 2 1

For Susan, Charlie and Braden,
I will love you and miss you until we meet again.

FOREWORD

No betrayal wounds more deeply than betrayal within a family.

There might be a way to finesse this, but Jennifer Graves doesn't, so I won't either: Her brother, Josh Powell, probably killed his wife Susan.

Jennifer feared Josh was responsible from the first moment her best friend and sister-in-law vanished. Her fear would be replaced by cold certainty with Josh's increasingly bizarre statements and actions that culminated, three years later, when he took an ax to his two boys and then consumed them all in an inferno.

To know that your brother did all that layers shame and disgust on top of grief. How do you survive such betrayal?

Jennifer survived by standing with Susan's family and condemning not only Josh, but also her father and other siblings who sought to shelter him and perhaps also hide his hideous crime.

She did it by holding tight to those around her. And she trusted both in the grace of God and His eternal and inescapable justice.

Ultimately, this is Jennifer's story of survival and redemption.

From those first panicked days of Susan Powell's disappearance in December of 2009, I covered the tragic story for television looking for glimmers of good that would somehow balance the overwhelming evil. Jennifer Graves is one of the lights I found in the cavernous dark.

Until this book, I did not understand the full, inside story of the anguish of those closest to Susan.

Jennifer shows us her journey from despair to resolve and finally hope in a deferred reunion in the world to come where Susan and her boys wait.

Brent Hunsaker
News Anchor, ABC 4 Utah

NOTE FROM THE AUTHORS

This book has been a healing and cathartic experience as I have taken the story that haunts me every day and put it onto paper. While I have tried to relate events in a manner that is factual as possible, I admit that this story is told from memory through the filter of my eyes, my heart and my experience. I do not claim to have every facet of every moment perfect and others may remember things in a different light.

In a few select cases, two separate conversations have been combined into one for ease of reading. Also, in order to protect their privacy, the names of several individuals have been changed. That being said, I am passionately committed to the account contained in these pages.

I pray with all my heart that those who are dealing with abuse and terror in their homes may find the courage to seek for help, stop the cycle and break free. May Susan's story teach us all to reach out to one another and to never, never give up.

PART ONE:
SEARCHING FOR SUSAN

"What we find changes who we become."
-Peter Morville

CHAPTER ONE

On February 5, 2012, news stations across the country blasted the image—a blackened shell of a house against a backdrop of Washington pine trees. Subtitles announced the information that Josh Powell, possible suspect in the disappearance of his wife, Susan Cox Powell, had taken the life of his two young sons, Charlie and Braden, in the most horrifying manner, ending his own life as well.

For me, this wasn't just a shocking news story. It was my family. Josh Powell was my brother. His most vocal supporter, Steve Powell, was my father. Their lies and slander had gone on for two years in front of the media. But it had gone on for decades for me.

I was in Utah, far away from the Washington scene. An empty set of bunk beds in an upstairs room and an extra-large van in the driveway both stood as testaments to the fact that I would not get the chance to raise Charlie and Braden, as I'd hoped.

The pain of living through this tragedy has often threatened to cripple me, yet I still stand strong in my faith. Somehow through the anxiety and fear, through the realization that my brother was a killer, I have been blessed with the peace that comes from knowing

God. I trust that one day justice will be done, but I refuse to let the waiting rob me of my peace.

Josh is now dead, along with his innocent boys. I can't mourn him yet. Maybe that day will come, but it's all still too new and fresh. For now, I can only think about his little family—his sweet, fun, sassy wife, Susan, who is still missing and presumed dead. His darling, vivacious boys, whom I had hoped to raise as my own. Loving them and losing them has changed me forever. They are the reason that this story needs to be told.

December 7, 2009

On that snowy, gray Monday morning, I was contemplating how relieved I was to be able to put the most difficult year of my life behind me. Everything had gone wrong over the last nine months, from money troubles to business failure to family drama and everything in between. But things were at last settling down. I was looking forward to focusing on caring for my five children, spending time with my husband, Kirk, and getting back on track with homeschool. I was ready to finally be free from crisis mode and to get ready for the holidays. So when Mom came upstairs to the kitchen with the phone in her hand, I wasn't prepared for the upheaval that followed.

"That was Debbie Caldwell," she said. We stood on either side of the counter. A few dishes were still in the sink from the night before, and I could hear my kids arguing upstairs. What a normal place for something so terrible to begin. "She said that Susan hasn't dropped off the boys. Debbie tried to call them, and even went over there and banged on the door. She hasn't been able to reach them." Mom's hazel eyes were distressed, and a sick feeling clamped down on my stomach. "She said there aren't any tracks in the snow in the driveway. They haven't gone anywhere this morning." Her voice trailed away.

"That's not like her," I said. My sister-in-law loved the boys' daycare provider like another grandma for her children. I couldn't think of any good reason she would stand Debbie up.

The kitchen tile was chilly against my bare feet, and I shivered as Mom and I spent a few minutes trying to reach either Susan or my brother, Josh. We dialed their cell phones, home phone, and work numbers. We couldn't reach anyone, and I knew right away we needed to get over to their house.

I called to the kids. "Hey, guys. Get dressed. We need to go to Uncle Josh's house. Hurry up," Then I scrambled to get a quick breakfast thrown together.

It didn't take long for us to all be ready, loaded in the minivan and on our way. A heavy storm during the night had dumped a thick blanket of white over everything. To this day, that is the image I see when I think of that first morning—the mounds of snow on either side of the road as we drove to their house. Mom and I continued to discuss the possible reasons for Susan's absence.

"Could it be carbon monoxide?" Mom asked, her voice low enough the children couldn't hear her. Her hands were clasped tightly in her lap and the distress practically oozed from her, seeping over me in cold waves.

I didn't want to consider it, but I couldn't keep the thought from taking root. Utah winters always brought that threat. The apprehension intensified. "Let's just get there and see what we can find." Mom nodded and stared out the window.

A few minutes later, we pulled into Sarah Circle and parked in front of the house. Susan and Josh had done a lot of work to the yard. In the spring, it would be heavily adorned with bright red tulips and a manicured lawn, a rustic wooden swing under a trellis. But for now, everything was obscured by the snow, the driveway perfectly smooth. A single set of footprints—, Debbie's, presumably—led to and from the front door. It was the only sign of life.

The house was a cute white rambler with a bay window in the living room and an attached two-car garage. All the blinds were closed up tightly, but that wasn't out of character. Mom and I went to the door, the kids following closely behind. We knocked and rang the bell, but were met only with silence. The nagging thought of carbon monoxide popped up again.

"Kristen, Jason, come here, please. I need you to climb the fence," I asked two of my children. They followed me to the side of the house, and Jason had a look of adventure on his nine-year-old face. I smiled, seeing this through his eyes—the brave explorer coming to the rescue.

"Check the doors and windows. If anything is open, go straight in and unlock the front door. Don't dawdle or mess around in there. Okay?" They both agreed, and I boosted them over the fence. They ran off around the yard, and I called to Mom, stationed at the front door, to watch for them. For a moment, I worried about what they could be exposed to, but my fears for them were unfounded. Everything was locked up tight.

I helped them scramble back over the fence and went to talk to Mom. She didn't speak any more words of anxiety, but her mouth was drawn in a tight line that I recognized at once. She was very concerned.

"Mom, we aren't getting anywhere. I don't know what else to do. I don't want to jump the gun, but I think we need to ˜all the police."

Part of me wanted her to argue, to tell me that I was overreacting, but she only nodded. "You're right." She dialed 911 and requested assistance. I listened for a moment, but my kids' voices carried across the silent yard, distracting me. We were obviously going to be here for a while, and it was extremely cold. I dialed my Aunt Lori's number.

Lori is only nine months older than me, and more like a sister. I explained the situation quickly and breathed a sigh of relief when she said she was willing to come and pick up the kids. At least they would be taken care of.

We huddled in the van, warming our hands in front of the vents and listening to the chatter of the kids in the back, while I tried Susan's work number again. Neither Mom nor I could remember the main numbers for Josh or Susan's employers; we only had numbers to their desks. One part of me wondered how silly I was going to feel when it turned out that they were at work this whole time, and that there had just been a mix-up with Debbie. The other part of me, however—the larger part—wanted to break that door down and call out the search parties. The dark feeling I'd had since seeing Mom on the phone that morning hadn't diminished. A weight descended on me, and with every passing minute, I was more and more convinced that something was seriously wrong.

Still, on the outside, I kept calm. My children were watching me, and so was Mom. I breathed quietly and deeply and tried to keep the worry from my face even as images of Charlie and Braden, my two adorable nephews, hovered in my mind.

I searched for something else I could do. I hadn't called my sister, Alina, yet. She and my dad and brothers were all in Washington, so there was nothing they could do to help. But at least she might be able to tell me if they'd heard from Josh. I dialed her cell phone number.

"Hi, it's Jenny. I'm wondering if you've heard from Josh or Susan today."

"No, why?"

I told her the details of the morning so far. "We were just wondering if Josh might have talked to Dad."

"I can ask him. Hold on." I was surprised by her response. I had expected my dad to be at work. Then it occurred to me that she might be calling him on their home phone. I couldn't hear anything in the background, so I wasn't sure if that was the case or if he really was at home.

"Dad said he talked to Josh for a few minutes yesterday at noon," she said a couple minutes later. "He said Josh called him to get a pancake recipe. We haven't heard from them since."

That was a little odd since Josh never cooked, but my mind was racing on to other things, like wondering when the police would get here and worrying about the boys.

"Okay. Let me know if you hear from him."

"Sure."

I went back to staring out the window and breathing. That was all I could do. It seemed like forever, but at last the police arrived, shortly followed by Lori. I hugged and kissed my kids quickly and sent them off in Lori's car, then turned my attention to the officer who had started to ask Mom some background questions.

It was a bit of a relief to have someone there in an official capacity. Somehow, it didn't feel quite so lonely. He listened patiently as we explained the situation.

A large, white van pulled up, and I spun around to see who it was, hoping for Susan's sunny face. It was Debbie Caldwell. She parked behind my car, hopped out, and hurried over to us, holding her coat tightly wrapped around her against the frigid morning.

"I only have a second, but I wanted to stop by and see if you'd found anything out." Her forehead was wrinkled with worry.

I shook my head. "No. We've been trying their cell phones and work numbers, but we can only reach their desks. I don't have numbers for their employers or for Chuck or Kiirsi." I had wanted to call Susan's dad and her best friend all morning.

"I have all those numbers. I've got a list for emergencies."

I laughed, a sharp sound without any amusement. "That appears to be what we have here."

The police officer came over to talk to Debbie and take down her statement. We got the numbers and Debbie waved, heading back to her car. "Keep me posted."

"I will," I said. I immediately tried Kiirsi's home and cell phone numbers, but they both went to voicemail. I left calm, detailed messages, but I wanted to scream. Wasn't there anyone who could help us make some progress?

Apparently, the police officer had more luck.

"I got through to both of their employers. Both were scheduled to come into work, but neither showed up or called in." He focused on me more intently, scribbling notes down with a new intensity. "I'm going to call for more assistance."

Mom and I exchanged a look. In one way, it was a relief to have him taking us more seriously. On the other hand, it was scarier than ever.

I chewed on the inside of my cheek and stared down the street, looking for the familiar blue Chrysler minivan Susan drove. There was nothing. The other houses on the circle were quiet with everyone off to work or at school. Somewhere close by, someone might know where Josh, Susan, and the boys were. Maybe someone had heard something in the night.

"I'm going to ask the neighbors if they've heard or seen anything," I called to Mom over my shoulder as I headed down the driveway.

One of the great things about being a Mormon in Utah is that if you knock on enough doors, you are sure to find a ward member. Wards are congregations based on geographical areas, so communities tend to be tight knit and friendly. I went to the first house and knocked. No one answered, but I kept trying. The first couple of people I found at home weren't acquainted with Josh and Susan any more than a wave in passing. But directly across the street, I found someone who could help me.

"Do you know the Powells? Josh and Susan?" I asked the woman who answered the door.

"I know Susan. Across the street, right?"

I nodded.

"Yes, they're in my ward."

"Oh, good." I sighed. "I'm Josh's sister, and I'm trying to track down anyone who might know where they are. Maybe the bishop or home teachers? And do you have Kiirsi Hellewell's address?"

"Sure, come in." She opened the door wider, and I stepped in to the welcome warmth of her living room. In a few moments, I had copied down the numbers for the church leaders who might have had contact with Susan. Josh was another story. I knew it had been quite a while since he had been to church regularly, even harping on Susan for her attendance. I gritted my teeth in frustration at this entire situation. He was so much like my dad.

"Thanks. I appreciate it." I stepped out onto her porch. The door closed behind me, but I didn't move. I was struck by the view of Josh and Susan's house, diagonally across the street. Mom was sitting in the car and the officer was pacing, talking on the phone. The reality, the gravity of the situation, slammed into me, weighing me down until I thought my knees might buckle. The thought kept running through my mind like ticker tape at the bottom of a news screen. *This is serious. This is serious. This is serious.*

It was time for me to call Chuck. I dialed his number with shaking hands. I didn't want to create a panic for Susan's parents. I cleared my throat a couple of times as the phone rang.

"Hi, Chuck," I said when he answered. "This is Jennifer, Josh's sister. I was wondering if you'd heard from Susan today."

"Oh, hi, Jennifer. No, we haven't heard from her for a couple of days. Is something wrong?"

Jennifer Graves and E. G. Clawson

What a loaded question. The evidence of a real problem was still a little sketchy, but the gnawing pain in my stomach said otherwise. "Well, she didn't drop the boys off with Debbie this morning. She didn't call her or anything, and neither of them showed up or called in to work today." I continued to describe the efforts we had made so far. "We called the police, and they just got here."

Chuck was quiet for a moment. I had tried to keep my voice calm, but I wondered if an edge of panic had crept in anyway. "Oh, okay." Another pause. "I'm sure they're fine. I talked to her a couple of days ago, and everything sounded okay. I'm sure they'll turn up any time."

I tried to let Chuck's calm voice soothe me, but I it wouldn't penetrate through the haze of doubt. I swallowed. "I hope so. Will you call me if you hear from her?"

"Of course. And let me know what else you find out."

"I will. Thanks, Chuck." I hung up the phone, and the shaking returned to my hands in full force.

Three more officers arrived shortly after I got back. They discussed the details that had been gathered so far, and their faces all wore matching grim expressions. One of them, a short, slight man with almost black hair, cleared his throat and turned toward Mom and me. "It sounds like we need to break in. We can do it if you will take responsibility for the broken window."

Mom and I agreed immediately.

The officers arranged themselves in front of the door, their postures poised and ready.

"Stay back. Don't come in unless I say it's clear," the tallest officer warned.

We nodded and hung back. The small officer broke the lower pane in the bay window nearest to the front door. He knocked out the broken shards of glass before he pushed the blinds aside and poked his head in.

I heard him mumble, "What's with the fans?" before climbing through the hole he had made. He opened the door, and the other officers walked inside, splitting up to search the house. I moved forward to stand right at the door. My heart hammered in my chest in fear at what they might find.

I noticed two big box fans running in the living room, but my eyes went past them immediately to the large birdcage near the dining room.

"Is the bird alive?" I called. The officer closest didn't seem to hear me; at least, he didn't answer. "Is the bird alive?" I asked again, more urgently.

"Yeah. It's alive," he called back, sounding annoyed. Instant relief flooded me. If the bird was alive, then my brother and his family weren't lying in their beds, dead from carbon monoxide poisoning.

Mom and I waited a couple more minutes while the officers did a quick search of the house.

"No one is here," the short officer said. He beckoned us inside. I stepped into the living room and headed down the hall to the bedrooms. The first door on the left was the boys' room. I glanced in as I passed. There were a few toys on the floor, nothing that appeared out of the ordinary. I didn't pause. Something pulled me further down the hall to Josh and Susan's room.

The officers continued to make a more thorough search, but I ignored them. My mind was buzzing with unanswered questions. Where were they? What would have caused them to leave so abruptly? I heard an officer say that the garage was empty. I shook my head and stepped inside the bedroom, hoping to find some kind of clue to their whereabouts.

There wasn't any obvious evidence that they'd packed for a trip. When I traveled, I always ended up with clothes and toiletries scattered around. But nothing appeared out of the ordinary. The bed was made, and there were typical personal belongings here and there. Susan's large deacon's bench occupied one wall. It had been a gift from her parents, and her name, Susan Marie Cox, was engraved above the dark green cushion. A couple of crochet projects rested on one end, half finished. Everything looked normal.

Then something else caught my eye. My chest constricted painfully as I walked around the bed toward a small table under the window.

Susan's purse.

I picked it up and sank down on the bed with it in my lap. I had a moment of guilt at the intrusion, but considering the fact that we had broken into her house, it was a small thing. With a deep breath, I yanked it open. I dug through it and found her keys and wallet. A lump rose in my throat. I swallowed past it and opened the wallet. Susan's blue eyes smiled up at me from her Driver's License. Credit cards and even her LDS temple recommend filled the slots.

I sat there with her keys in one hand and her wallet in the other, and the questions were inevitable. Where on earth would Susan go without her wallet or keys? Without calling in to work or letting Debbie know? My hands started to shake, causing the keys to jingle, and I put everything back in the purse quickly as an officer spoke from the living room.

"The carpets have just been cleaned," he said.

The air rushed out of me like I'd been punched in the stomach.

He's done something to her, I thought. And the nightmare began.

CHAPTER TWO

I walked out into the hall. My legs felt like lead.

"Susan's purse is still here." I handed the purse to the nearest officer and moved woodenly to the living room, where Mom and the other officers had converged. I wanted to throw up, but I tamped the emotion down and sealed it behind a calm face. *I don't know anything for sure. I don't want to start a witch hunt*, I thought. One look at Mom's pale face and I knew I was right to keep my thoughts to myself. For now.

Debbie Caldwell knocked on the open door.

"Hi, Debbie," I said, walking over to her. "They aren't here. The car's not in the garage." *Susan's purse is here.* The words wouldn't come out. They were stuck, trapped under the lump in my throat.

Debbie sighed and closed her eyes for a second. When she opened them, they went straight to the broken window. "I feel so stupid. I have a key. I didn't even think . . . it never occurred to me that you would have to break in."

Debbie was twisting her fingers together over and over. I put my hand on hers to stop the frantic movement. "We didn't, either. It's okay. I'm only surprised Josh let you have a key."

Jennifer Graves and E. G. Clawson

"Oh, he didn't know about it. Susan gave it to me in case he locked her out again. She swore me to secrecy. I couldn't tell a soul, or Josh might have found out and changed all the locks on the house just to spite her. He was so paranoid!" She shrugged apologetically and handed me the key. "Just in case you need to get back in." I imagined what this situation must be like for her, standing here saying something unflattering about my brother to my face. I patted her hand and leaned against the door. The cold wind felt good on my face. At least it reminded me that there was a world outside of this little, empty house.

The suspicions I had were so newly formed, I couldn't quite put shape or meaning to them, but Debbie's comment added weight. I wondered if I should say something about it to the police.

"I'll keep you posted, okay?" How many times had I made that promise already this morning?

Debbie nodded, gave me a quick, tight smile, and headed back to her car.

I closed the door softly and went back to sit by Mom on the couch. My phone rang before I could relax against the cushions. It was Kiirsi, returning my call. I gave her a quick update, and she murmured her concern.

"I talked to another lady in the ward. Jovanna Owing," Kiirsi said. "She told me she was here with Susan and Josh yesterday. She came over to help Susan with untangling some yarn. I guess that they went to Josh's company Christmas party on Saturday. She said they won a video camera. Maybe the police should talk to her. I can get her number for you."

The short police officer came into the room, and I passed the information along. Mom leaned forward, listening intently. The mention of the camera sparked something in her. I could see a new idea forming. She didn't say anything about it until I'd hung up with Kiirsi. Then it came rushing out.

"They could have gone for a drive," Mom said. "Josh has always loved taking pictures. Maybe they took the video camera and went up through the canyon. They could have slid off the side of the road. For all we know, they are lying in a ditch somewhere, freezing to death."

She spoke quietly, her voice catching at the end, and leaned forward to rub her leg. I almost wished her idea was right. It would be so much better than what I had been thinking.

How could it be possible, though? A sense of disorienting unreality washed over me. It was impossible that I was sitting in Josh and Susan's house thinking that he could have harmed her, but that awful feeling had been stronger and stronger ever since we had received Debbie's first call that morning. Seeing Susan's purse, knowing the carpets had been cleaned—all the little circumstances left me feeling like I was watching a murder mystery unfold on a television screen. Once again, an image of Charlie and Braden, giggling as they wrestled with my boys, popped into my head. Where were the boys? If Josh really had done something . . . what about them?

I got up and started pacing, too antsy to sit still. I wished Kirk were here. But he was out of town on business, and he hadn't returned my voicemail yet. I wanted to talk to him so badly, to have him reassure me that everything was going to be okay. That my worries were all in my head.

I wandered through the kitchen, randomly opening cupboard doors, then went over to the door off the dining room. I opened it and looked out into the garage. It was clean and organized and completely dry. It was obvious that they hadn't been here since last night, or there would have been melted snow in puddles on the floor. I sighed and closed the door, then went back to the living room.

The bird caught my attention. It was a pathetic thing—a green and yellow parrot of some sort with most of its feathers pulled out on the lower half of its body. It had been beautiful until Charlie was born. Then, as Josh and Susan's attention turned to their new baby, the parrot had started to show signs of distress. I felt as raw and exposed as the bird. I watched it absently, overwhelmed by my own helplessness. What could I do besides sit here and wait for them to come home?

No, I couldn't even do that.

An officer came back to the living room. "We need to do a preliminary search of the house, and no one can be on the premises.

13

We'll contact you as soon as we hear anything." They were kicking us out.

I sighed. "Okay," I said. "Mom?"

Mom looked around the room and nodded woodenly. We went out the front door, and the officer followed behind us.

"I have one more quick question before you go," the officer said. I stopped and turned back, Mom beside me. "Is there any history of violence between your brother and his wife?"

It was a simple question and not unexpected in a case like this, I was sure. But I felt the force of it pressing me down into the ground and Mom's tension ratcheting up a notch. I cleared my throat. "Well, not really violence. They were having trouble. And he did hit her once."

I explained the incident quickly. It was a little more than a year earlier. Susan had called and asked Mom and me to come over. She and Josh had been in a fight, and she wanted us to talk to him. I couldn't even remember what they'd been fighting about, though I thought it was a conversation between Josh and my dad that had set him off, which wasn't unusual—only that time, Susan had been mad enough to hit Josh, and he had hit her back. She was pretty shaken up.

I wasn't sure what she'd wanted me to say. Josh was in the wrong, for sure, and Mom had tried and tried to talk some sense into him, but Susan was at fault, too. I pulled her into the other room.

"Don't hit him again. It's not okay. Besides, you don't want to go there. That's a door that should stay closed—he's always going to be stronger than you." I didn't want her to give him an excuse to hit her. As far as I knew, that was the only time. But I had to wonder, had I done the wrong thing back then? Should I have counseled her to leave him? I've asked myself that same question so many times since then. I still don't have an answer.

The officer jotted down notes as I rehearsed the story. The disapproval radiated from Mom. I glanced at her out of the corner of my eye. Her jaw was clamped, and her mouth was a thin line. She wouldn't look at me. I tried to see this from her perspective as a protective mother. I needed to be patient with her.

By the time we got home, it was late afternoon. Lori had things under control with the kids, and I sat down at the kitchen table. All of the stress of the morning came crashing in at once, and I didn't know if I'd ever be able to move from this table again. Mom and Lori sat across from me, and we all stared at each other. None of us had the energy to speak. Or maybe we simply didn't know what to say. My ear was tuned to the sound of the phone. Part of me longed for it to ring, but the rest of me dreaded it. I couldn't think of a single scenario where we would be getting good news, but I also couldn't wait for Kirk to call.

I took a deep breath. My cousin Jessica had been weighing on my mind. I figured Lori had let her know what was going on, but I needed to talk to her. She loved Susan, too. I dialed her number.

"I'm coming to stay with you," were the first words out of her mouth. A tiny crack appeared in the wall holding my emotions at bay, and I sighed in relief. Jes was dealing with her own struggles. She was separated from her husband, caring for her one-year-old son Garrin on her own, and living with her dad. It wasn't an ideal situation, but she was there for me anyway. She knew exactly what I needed.

"Thank you. I'd really like that." I filled her in on the scanty details of the morning.

She stayed quiet through the short recitation, but I could hear the emotion in her voice. "I'm sure they'll turn up and everything will be fine." Did she know she sounded as unconvinced as I felt? "I'll get down there somehow. I don't have a car right now . . . "

"Maybe Lori could pick you and Garrin up," I said. Lori, listening in, nodded in agreement. "Lori says yes. Here, talk to her." I passed the phone over to Lori, and they made arrangements. Lori was out the door in just a few minutes.

When the phone rang again a few minutes later, I must have jumped a foot in my chair. I glanced at the caller ID and breathed a sigh of relief, then snatched up the phone and flipped it open.

"Kirk," I said. "You got my message?"

"Yes, are you okay?" The simple sound of his voice made me relax enough to let the words come that I had been holding in since we got home. I started to walk upstairs with the phone, away from my mother's listening ears. I wasn't ready to share my fears with her. Not until I knew more.

"I'm fine, but they weren't at the house." I detailed the efforts we had made in trying to reach either of them, and the fact that they hadn't gone to work or called in. I told him about calling the police and what they had found. "The car hasn't been there all night. Susan's purse was sitting in her room with her wallet and keys still in it. And the carpets had just been cleaned. There were fans blowing in the living room to dry them out." I closed the door to my room and lowered my voice. "Kirk, I think Josh has done something to Susan." There. I had said it out loud.

Kirk was quiet for a moment. "What do the police think?" he asked.

"They didn't really say anything about it. They are doing a preliminary search, and they said they were going to leave an officer at the house because of the broken window. But my guess is that they are waiting for Josh to come home. I'm sure they're suspicious. How could they not be?"

"And what about your mom? What does she say about all of this?"

"I haven't told her my worry yet. She thinks they've been in a car accident somewhere and are freezing to death on the side of the road."

"It's a possibility, I guess."

"As far as I'm concerned, that would be better than the alternative, but I don't believe it. Kirk, I think Josh has done something horrible." The emotional dam burst. My voice cracked, and for the first time that day, I started to cry.

"Jenny," Kirk said, his voice soothing. "You don't know that. I won't pretend to like Josh, but I can't think he would actually harm Susan. For one thing, it seems far too proactive for him."

I laughed, a short little burst of amusement amid the bleakness that was washing over me.

Kirk went on. "Let the police handle it. I'm sure they're doing everything they can do. For now, let's try to assume the best. Maybe they *were* in a car accident, but that doesn't mean they're dead. We have to hope they'll turn up and everything will be okay."

16

I let Kirk's comforting words wrap around me, a warm embrace that eased the worry and fear for a moment.

"Thank you, honey. I love you," I said when I had calmed down.

"I love you, too. I have to get back to class, but I'll call you later. Let me know if you hear anything from the police, okay?"

"Okay." I was quiet.

"Jenny?"

"I just wish you were here," I said, the tears coming close to the surface again.

"Me, too. But I'll be home on Wednesday. Hang in there, honey. You are strong."

"I know. But I don't want to be," I said, letting a little bit of peevishness enter my voice.

He laughed. "I know." There was another pause. "Sweetie, I have to go. I'll call you later, okay?"

"Okay, bye."

"Bye." I hung up and stared at the phone in my hand. The comfort of Kirk's words started to fade all too soon.

CHAPTER THREE

Someone in my ward apparently heard what was going on. A little later, I got a call from a neighbor offering to bring dinner over. It was a small thing, but the simple act of caring by a friend meant a lot to me. It was one less thing for me to worry about.

Mom and I sat in the living room. My kids were sprawled around the family room, playing with Lori's kids—Legos and Polly Pockets and craft projects all thrown into the mix. Abigail kept bringing her Polly Pockets to me to put little outfits on and take them off again. I tried to stay calm and patient with her, but I wanted to throw the tiny plastic doll across the room in frustration. It wasn't her fault, though. I complied, a smile plastered on my face, and Abigail responded with her own beautiful five-year-old grin.

My call with Kirk had eased my mind somewhat. I was still fighting with that black feeling, but I knew he was right. There was nothing else I could do but try to hope for the best and wait to hear from the police.

And I prayed. Silently, desperately, I pleaded with God to keep them all safe.

I had been instructed to call the police if we heard anything from Josh or Susan, and they had promised they would do the same. I played with the phone while I chatted with Mom. Every once in a while I would glance down at it, hoping to see a number that could be the police calling.

There was a knock at the door, and my heart started to pound. Maybe they would come to the door if it was really bad news.

"I'll get it," Jeffrey, my oldest son, said, running in from the family room. I glanced at Mom and could see the same tension in her face.

"Hi there," a cheerful voice said from the porch. It was my neighbor, heavily laden with covered baking dishes. I stood up and went to the door, trying to keep a pleasant expression on my face.

"Thanks so much for dinner. You didn't have to do that," I said. I talked with her for a minute about the morning, updating her on the basic events so far. "So we are just waiting to hear."

My cell phone rang. I glanced at the number: it was Alina. She had called a number of times through the afternoon, being unusually talkative. Mom came over to chat with the neighbor. I waved at them and mouthed "thank you" as I hit the button to answer the call.

"Hi, Alina. We still haven't heard anything. The police asked us to leave so they could search the house. We haven't heard anything from them since."

"What do we do?"

"Not much we can do. At this point, we can only wait for them to show up or at least call."

As if on cue, the home phone rang. I walked over to the phone and looked at the caller ID, expecting it to be the police or maybe Kirk. When I saw the number, I was stunned.

It was Josh.

"Hold on, it's Josh! I'll call you back," I said to Alina. I flipped the cell phone closed and grabbed the handset. "Hello?"

"Hello."

My heart was hammering in my ears.

"Josh? Where are you? We've been looking for you all day! Are Susan and the boys with you?

Mom turned around at my words, a look of relief washing over her face.

"The boys are with me. I'm at Susan's work. I came to pick her up, but she's not here." I couldn't believe how unemotional he sounded.

"What do you mean? Where have *you* been? Isn't she with you?" I fired the questions at him, nearly yelling. What would he be doing at Susan's work? It was a blatant lie.

"What do you know?" he asked, the first real concern coming through in his voice.

"I, um . . . wait. What?"

"They said she didn't show up today."

What had he said? I drew another breath and was about to light into him, to grill him about Susan's whereabouts, but a thought came to me so forcibly it sucked the wind out of me. *Calm down and back off or he will run with the boys.* It was almost like I had heard a voice inside my head. I took another deep breath, this time to calm myself.

"I'm glad to hear you're okay. We were worried about you, Josh," I said. "We even called the police, and they had to break a window to get in." I thought about the patrol car sitting outside of the house. Would he take off if he saw it? "They left an officer there to keep an eye on the house, you know, just in case someone tried to take advantage of that broken window."

"Okay."

That was it. No emotion again.

"Mom's been so worried. She wants to see you. Can we meet at your house?"

"Sure."

I waited, unsure of what else to say. Josh still didn't mention Susan at all.

"Well, we'll head over there now," I said.

"Okay. Bye."

I hung up the phone and stared at it. Fear and disbelief boiled inside of me, and I was more certain than ever that he was responsible. The idea that Josh was trying to pick Susan up at work when we all knew for a fact that she hadn't been there . . . it was ridiculous. What about the fact that he hadn't shown up for work

21

today? And where was his concern for his wife? Where was the worry? There had been no emotion, nothing.

Mom was waiting for me to say something. She had gathered already from my yelling that Susan wasn't with him. I glanced up at her, and I just couldn't bring myself to share my fears. This was her son.

I cleared my throat. "Josh and the boys are going to meet us at the house," I said.

"What about Susan?" Mom asked.

The words hung there for a minute, and I simply shook my head.

"I'll go get my coat." Mom went into the other room.

I dialed the phone quickly. "Hi, Jes. Josh just called. He says he doesn't know where Susan is." I told her the story about supposedly trying to pick her up at work.

"Yeah, right." Her voice was thick with anger. It sounded the way I felt, only she didn't have to put on a show.

"Exactly," I whispered. "How far away are you? I need to go meet him at his house."

"We're only a few minutes away. Ten, maybe. Will the kids be okay until we get there?"

"Yes, Jeffrey and Kristen can watch the little ones for that long. Thanks, Jes."

I had one more call to make.

"Hi, Alina. That was Josh just now."

"Oh, good. What did he say?" I couldn't help feeling that her relief was misplaced.

"Well, he claims he doesn't know where Susan is. He said he went to pick her up from work, but she wasn't there."

I could tell instantly that I had said something wrong. I scanned back over my words—"he claims." The resentment that was flooding through the phone was palpable. *I shouldn't have said that*, I thought. But I couldn't call it back. I tried to gloss over it instead.

"Mom and I are going over there to see what we need to do to help. I'll tell him to call you, ok?"

"Thanks."

I sincerely hoped that little slip wouldn't cause problems later on.

"Jeffrey, Kristen," I called to my two oldest. They came upstairs, and I spoke quickly, keeping my voice down so the little ones wouldn't hear. "Uncle Josh just called. I need to go over there. Lori and Jessica are on their way back. They'll be here in a few minutes. Can you watch your brothers and sister and cousins until they get back?"

They must have seen that this wasn't necessarily good news. Their eyes were big and troubled. I gave them each a hug and kiss. "Be good and help with the kids tonight, okay? I'm not sure how late I'll be." I gave them each one more quick hug and hurried off to get my own coat.

Susan's work was only ten to fifteen minutes away from their house, so we needed to hurry. I wanted to see Josh. Maybe I'd be able to tell for sure what had happened simply by looking into his face.

CHAPTER FOUR

I called the police on the way to the house. My hands shook as I dialed the phone, but I knew what I had to do. I still wasn't sure how much of my suspicion I should share with them but I certainly was going to do everything I could to help find the truth.

I was referred to Detective Maxwell, who had been assigned as the lead investigator in the case.

"Josh just called me and said he has the boys. Susan isn't with him," I said. I told Maxwell about Josh's claim that he had been at Susan's work, trying to pick her up. "He's going to meet us at the house. I wanted to let you know." I wasn't sure what else to say.

"We have an officer there right now. I'll meet you there as well. Just do one thing. When he gets there, stay in your car unless I say it's clear."

I agreed, but my tension ratcheted up a bit. I hung up and glanced at Mom.

"Are the police going to be there?" she asked. "What are their plans?"

"I'm not sure. I think there is still an officer there from earlier. I guess we'll have to wait and see."

I expected to see the patrol car when we arrived, but there was also another, unmarked vehicle. Detective Maxwell had beat us there.

He got out of the car and walked toward us. Maxwell was tall and broad shouldered with dark blond hair. He wore simple khakis, a button-down shirt, and a jacket, but he walked with the authority of someone who knew how to handle anything. I felt a little more relaxed knowing he was in control of the situation.

"Jennifer?" he asked when I rolled down my window. I nodded. "Have you heard anything else from your brother?"

"No. He just said he'd meet us here. Susan's work is only ten minutes or so away. He should be here soon."

Maxwell nodded and went back to his car.

We waited for a half an hour, a full hour after our last conversation, and Josh still hadn't shown up.

"I'm going to call him and find out where he is," I told Mom.

I dialed his number, and it rang through to voicemail.

"This is ridiculous. If he was at Susan's work, he'd be here by now," I said.

"Maybe the traffic is bad," Mom said.

I shook my head. Not bad enough for it to take him an hour to get here. I already knew he'd been lying about picking up Susan, but this made me even more anxious to know where he actually was. Had I scared him? Did he run? My heart raced at a painful rate as I thought about Charlie and Braden, alone and defenseless.

My phone rang, and I snatched it up and answered it.

"Sorry, we're running late. I decided to stop and get pizza," Josh said.

"We've been waiting for an hour, Josh," I said, exasperation coloring my voice. I wanted to grill him, but that same feeling from earlier restrained me, and I spoke more calmly. "Just hurry up, okay?"

"Yeah," he said. That was it.

Detective Maxwell saw me hang up the phone, and he came back to the window. "Was that him?"

"Yes. He said something about stopping to get pizza for the boys," I said. I couldn't keep the skepticism out of my voice. Maxwell glanced at his watch and shook his head.

"Call him back, please," he said.

I dialed the phone and placed it in his outstretched hand.

"Yes, this is Detective Maxwell with the West Valley City Police department. We are waiting at your home with your sister and mother. We'd like to speak to you."

I could hear the murmur of Josh's voice on the other end of the call, something about pizza again.

Detective Maxwell shook his head and spoke firmly. "No, you need to get back here." There was no room for argument in his voice. He ended the call and handed the phone back to me. I wanted to say something to him about my suspicions, but Mom's presence next to me felt like a muzzle. I didn't want to freak her out. I kept my mouth shut and watched as he returned to his car. The unspoken words threatened to choke me.

The longer we waited, the more I thought about the boys. I couldn't help wondering what Charlie and Braden must be going through. Were they okay? Something kept my mind carefully insulated from asking the same questions about Susan.

It was at least twenty minutes more before headlights shone around the corner, announcing Josh's arrival. As soon as Mom saw it was him, she started to open her door.

"Mom! Stay in the car!" I blurted. "I forgot to tell you. Maxwell said not to get out until he says it's okay." Mom stared at Josh's van and back at me. I could see the conflict in her eyes—her need to make sure he was okay warring with her desire to follow the instructions of the police. It was a quiet battle, over quickly, and she got back in, closing the door softly.

I rolled down the window, letting in the icy blast of winter wind, and watched as Maxwell got out of his car and approached Josh's van resolutely. Seeing him take the situation so seriously made it even more surreal.

We were too far away to hear them speaking, but I could see their postures, calm and in control on both sides. I squinted, wishing I could see Josh's face, look into his eyes. My earlier desire to decipher his guilt was still strong, but I stayed obediently in the car. I only hoped that Maxwell would be able to see what I could not.

I tore my glance away from him and looked over the rest of Josh's car. The front passenger seat was obviously empty. The back was obscured by tinted windows and the darkness, but I thought I could make out two little heads barely poking above the backs of the car seats. I wanted to go and pull the boys from the back of the car and take them home with me, wrap them up safely, away from all the frightening tension that was building.

My eyes swerved back to Josh as he rolled up his window and Maxwell went back to his car. Mom and I watched in frustration as Josh backed up and headed out of the circle, followed by the patrol car.

Maxwell pulled up next to our car and rolled his window down. "We are going back to the station to ask him some questions."

The suspicions that I had been swallowing for the past few hours bubbled up, and I couldn't hold them back any longer.

"This doesn't look right," I blurted. "Where has he been for the past two hours that we've been waiting for him? Taking all that time to get pizza—I don't buy it. *Where is Susan?*" I demanded. I knew I was starting to sound hysterical, but I couldn't help it. Mom sucked in a sharp breath next to me, but I ignored her. "What has he done?" I said, the words coming out in a breathy whoosh.

"That is what we are trying to find out," Maxwell said calmly. His manner was confident and forceful, and it reassured me some. "You can wait here if you like, but I don't know how long we'll be."

I glanced at Mom, pale and tense beside me. My protective instinct resurfaced, taking the wind out of my sails.

I sighed. "No, we'll go home. But please, will you call me if you need me to come and pick up the boys?"

"Sure," he said. He nodded once and then pulled away. I watched his tail lights until they disappeared around the corner.

The exhaustion of the day slammed into me all at once, leaving me slumped and shaken. It had been one long, torturous round of phone calls and waiting, and we still had nothing to show for it.

That wasn't entirely true. I knew that my brother wasn't telling the truth. Two hours to pick up pizza when his wife had been reported missing? It was ridiculous, as was his claim to not know where Susan was. I had the horrible feeling it was just the first hint of more lies to come.

CHAPTER FIVE

That night, I dreamed about Susan. She was trying to call me, but I could never get to the phone in time. I woke up in a panic, my heart pounding out of my chest as I truly accepted for the first time that Susan was probably dead. I wanted to go back to sleep, thinking that maybe Susan's spirit could tell me where her body was. It was an idea that haunted me for months.

I had come home the night before with the idea that the police would be calling me to come pick up the boys at any time. I stayed up late making phone calls and talking to Kirk on the phone. It had been hard to fall asleep, and I was exhausted.

Another storm had rolled through during the night, and a glance out of the window showed how deep the snow was. I dreaded going out in the cold, but I was determined to do whatever I had to do to help with the boys, so I got bundled up for the day, and Mom and I headed out the door as soon as we could get everything settled.

It was wonderful having Jessica there. I was relieved to let her deal with watching the kids—and all the other things that I usually did as a mom—but even more than that, I needed the emotional support that only a dear friend could give. She understood that there was no room in my mind for anything other than Susan and the boys, and she did everything she could to lift my burden.

It was just as well that we got on the road so early. What had been a twenty minute drive yesterday was going to take double or triple that amount of time today. Cars were sliding all over the icy, snowy roads, and we made our way at a white-knuckled crawl. We were only halfway there when Josh called.

"Can you come watch the boys?" he asked. "I need to go in to talk to the police at ten."

I glanced at the clock. "I'll try, but we are barely going to make it by then. The roads are horrible."

"That's okay. Whenever you get here is fine," he said nonchalantly.

"Well, we're on our way," I said.

It was close to ten when we arrived. I hurried to the front door, eager to see Charlie and Braden for the first time since everything had happened. I knocked and waited. Josh answered dressed in a holey t-shirt and jeans, hardly ready for an interview. As we entered, I was surprised to find the boys playing in the living room with broken glass still on the floor under the window. I figured Josh had been so busy getting ready to leave that he hadn't had time to clean up the glass, or maybe hadn't noticed. That idea was negated a moment later when I saw the piece of cardboard he had wedged in the window to replace the broken pane.

And Josh *wasn't* ready to go. He hadn't even taken a shower or changed his clothes or anything. He was wandering around, puttering and straightening the house.

What had he been doing all morning?

"Josh, don't you need to go?" I asked. I didn't want to grill him and mess up what the police were going to be doing in their interview, but I wanted him to get to the station so they could do their job.

"Yeah, but the boys haven't had breakfast," he said. He looked flustered.

"That's okay," Mom said. "We'll make breakfast. You go get ready."

"Yeah, in a minute."

Mom and I took the boys into the kitchen, and Josh went out to the garage. I peeked around the corner, watching as he went through the back garage door into the yard and came in with an armful of wet towels and rags. What had he been doing with them in the backyard . . . in the winter . . . the morning after his wife went missing? He carried them into the laundry room to start a load of wash. Bile rose up in my throat at the sight. How was I supposed to handle this situation? Was Josh destroying evidence? If so, it was too late for me to stop that load of laundry. The least I could do was take in all the information I could and share it later with the police. I glanced around the garage. It had been perfectly clean the day before. Now the floor was covered in puddles of water, and sawdust was scattered all over.

I glanced to the side and saw a sled that was covered in a pile of stuff, tools and work gloves on top. I didn't have much time to look it over, only to notice that it definitely hadn't been here the day before. But Josh was close by, and I didn't want to tip him off to my suspicion. I went back into the house and tried to keep my face calm.

Detective Maxwell called and asked if we were at Josh's house, and if Josh was still there.

"He hasn't left yet." *And he's doing laundry, and there's weird stuff in the garage.* I couldn't exactly share the details with Josh listening in.

"Tell him I'm waiting to talk to him. He needs to get in here."

"I will." I hung up and relayed the message. Josh just nodded. A horrible, disorienting feeling spread through me. On one hand, I was becoming more and more certain that I was dealing with a murderer, and yet . . . this was the familiar face of my brother. I couldn't make the two images gel into one person.

My heart raced, and I forced myself to ask the question I'd been screaming silently for the last twenty-four hours. "Josh, do you know where Susan is?"

"No, I haven't seen her."

"Where were you and the boys, then?" I tried to keep my voice conversational and politely interested.

"We went camping and saw some sheep and stuff." That was it. I mentally laughed at that claim. *Camping? In January? In a snow storm with a two- and four-year-old? Yeah, right.*

"Um, you really should probably get going. Mom and I'll take care of things here, okay?" I bent down to start picking up glass.

"Just leave that," Josh said. "They need breakfast."

That made no sense, but I backed away. "Sure, yeah. We'll make sure they eat."

"Okay. I'm going to go take a shower." He went down the hall, and I took a deep breath for the first time since arriving.

"Come on, boys. Let's go have some breakfast," I said.

Charlie bounded around the kitchen, full of his usual energy. It was compounded, in fact, by the lack of his normal routine. Braden was quiet and came in to eat. Mom had finished cooking and dished them each up a plate, and we sat them down at the table. I tried to examine their faces, to see any hints there of what might have happened over the last two days. After they ate, we went in the living room to play.

"Charlie, did you go camping with Daddy?" I asked, smoothing his hair. He didn't say anything, just stared at his toys. I listened for the shower, afraid Josh would come out and hear me questioning his boys. The sound of running water continued. "Charlie," I asked, "where's your mom?"

"At work," he said.

"Did you go camping the other night?"

"No. Daddy said no s'mores." Charlie was matter of fact as he pushed a car along the carpet. "We saw police, though," he said in his little voice. "It was big. And we had pizza." He continued to chat about the big police station, but I couldn't get any more information about the supposed camping trip. Then the water shut off in the bathroom, and I didn't dare to question him anymore while Josh was still there.

When he came down the hall, finally dressed and ready to go, Mom offered Josh some breakfast, but he refused. He glanced around, and I knew we had to get him out of the house.

"What else can we do to help you?" I asked.

"Do the dishes. And laundry would be good, and just . . . clean up."

"Sure," Mom said. "We'll take care of it. Are you sure you don't want to eat?" I wanted to shush her, but Josh went into the kitchen and ate a few bites.

32

"I guess I'd better get going," he said. It was almost noon, two hours after he was supposed to be at the police station. *Hardly a grieving or worried husband anxious to help find his missing wife,* I thought. I held my breath until he was out of the house. Then I ran to the window and watched him drive away.

I let out a sigh of relief and hurried to clean up the broken glass.

CHAPTER SIX

After I got the boys dressed, I came out of their room to see that Mom had started doing the dishes.

"Why don't you work on the laundry and the boys' room, and I'll finish up the kitchen and vacuum," she suggested.

"No, Mom. I don't think we should be cleaning. That doesn't feel like a good idea."

"Why not?"

I stared at her, not sure what to say. *Because this could be a crime scene. Because your son may be a murderer!* The words boiled in my brain, but I kept them locked inside. "Why don't we at least ask the police if it's okay?"

"If you think we need to," Mom said. She called Detective Maxwell, and I started to walk through the house again, looking for any details that might help the police.

The upstairs was pretty much as it had been the other day. Nothing seemed out of place other than the towels, the glass from the broken window, and the mess in the garage. I went downstairs into the basement. It was mostly unfinished, with only one room walled in that Josh used for an office. I glanced in there, but didn't see anything. As I walked into the storage room, I spotted a box that caught my attention.

I crouched down and opened it. It was full of some of Susan's memorabilia from her teenage years. There were a couple of old photo albums on top, and I glanced through them briefly. My hands started to shake again.

"Oh, Susan. Where are you?" My voice echoed against the barren concrete walls.

I heard the dishwasher start, and I ran upstairs. Mom saw my anxious expression and hurried to reassure me.

"Maxwell said whatever we want to do is fine," she said. I was surprised, but shrugged, and she went back to cleaning the kitchen. The boys and I read a few stories, and Mom swapped out a load of laundry. Fifteen minutes or so later, the doorbell rang.

Two detectives stood on the porch, a man and a woman.

"I'm Detective Petersen. We have a warrant to search the house," the man said, holding up a piece of paper. My heart dropped. I *knew* we shouldn't have been cleaning.

"We did some cleaning. Detective Maxwell said it was okay and . . ." I stumbled over my words in a rush to explain.

"Okay. But we do need to search the house again. I'm sorry, but you can't be on the premises. Take your time getting your things together, and get whatever you need for the boys." He was scrupulously polite. There was no sense of trust there, no confiding any details forthcoming from them. It was a very strange feeling. They weren't going to tell us that we were doing anything wrong, or ask us to do anything to help them. They didn't know where I stood or if I was going to try to help Josh cover anything up, so they wouldn't put any requests or information in my lap. I knew I was firmly on their side, but they didn't. Mom and I exchanged looks, but we both went into the boys' room to gather up clothes and a few toys. While Mom was busy with the boys, I had to take the opportunity to share my concerns with the police.

I hurried back to the living room where they were waiting patiently.

"Look, while I have the boys with me, it's an opportunity. If you want to talk to them and ask them any questions, now would be the time to do it. I'd be happy to take them wherever you need." I gave them my cell phone number and willed them to understand what I was saying. *I know Josh is guilty of some crime. I want to help.*

"Thanks. We'll call you if it's needed." That was it. I wanted to shout at them, but I only nodded once, then left the detectives to their search. Mom and I loaded the boys into the car and got them buckled into the car seats.

"You guys want to come play at my house with your cousins?" I asked.

"Yay!" Charlie cheered, making Braden giggle.

"Come on then, let's go," I said. I looked back at the detectives standing on the porch and hesitated for a minute. I desperately wanted them to know that they could trust me. Besides, if I didn't tell them my fears, I was going to explode. I hesitated, glancing back at Mom, then straightened my shoulders and marched back to the house.

"I don't want to say this in front of my mother. She has a tendency to be a bit overprotective. But I have to tell you, I think that Josh has done something to Susan. He hasn't been acting normally. Everything is suspicious." I couldn't keep the emotion out of my voice. "Just be thorough, okay? I'm really worried." That was as much as I could say, but Detective Petersen's face softened ever so slightly.

"We appreciate you sharing your concerns. We'll be in touch if we need anything more." There was still no information, but at least they knew where I stood. I could only hope it would lead to more in the future.

"That's all I ask," I said.

As we started for home, I called Jes to check on my kids and let her know we were headed home. I had barely hung up with her when the phone rang. It was the female detective.

"Jennifer, we actually would like to have you take the boys to the Children's Justice Center, if you don't mind."

I wanted to do a little victory dance. At last, they were putting a little trust in me, knowing that I was going to follow through and do something they were asking me to do. Everything about this situation up till now had left me powerless, but this was an action I could take.

"Absolutely. Give me the address and we'll go right now." I repeated it out loud so Mom could jot it down, then we turned and headed straight there. I called Jes to let her know our change of plans. She was as pleased as I was with this development.

Next, I called Chuck to give him an update. We exchanged brief pleasantries, but they were stilted, mere habit. I told him about Josh's interview and where I was taking the boys.

"Josh just called me to finally inform me that my daughter has been missing since yesterday." His voice was thick with disgust. I flinched at yet another sign of Josh's guilt.

"Wow. He didn't even call you last night?"

"Nope."

There was a sense of restraint between us. I tried to see it from Chuck's perspective. Talking to me, Josh's sister, probably didn't feel very safe to him right now. I wanted him to know that I was on his side. He had no one else who could let him know what was going on, and Susan was, after all, his daughter. But I didn't quite know what to say.

"I'll try to keep you posted on what happens. But for now, the boys are safe with me."

It was all I could think of, but I could almost feel a sense of softening on the other end of the line, like with Detective Peterson, maybe a beginning of trust. We said goodbye, and I turned my attention back to the drive and the boys.

The Children's Justice Center in West Jordan was a bit of a surprise. It didn't look like a big government facility, more like a small office building. The receptionist was kind and took down our information. We took a seat in the waiting room. Bookcases filled with storybooks, bins of small toys, dollhouses, and big trucks all filled the space. Through the large windows, I could see a play area outside. It was all designed to make a child feel comfortable and relaxed. The boys played for only a few minutes before a woman came to get Charlie.

"Are you Charlie?" she asked, then introduced herself. She was pleasant and obviously had a way with children. "Would it be all right if you came back and talked with me? You could see our other toy room."

Charlie considered her words for a second and glanced back at me, then nodded and stood to take her hand. Mom and I watched him disappear around the corner, walking down the hall. I found myself reaching for my wedding ring and spinning it around and around, a nervous habit.

We weren't told what was revealed, but Charlie seemed fine and happy when he came back out.

The woman tried to talk to Braden casually, but he was too little to show any interest. That didn't bother her at all. She was kind and gave us some information about caring for children who are going through trauma.

"Sometimes kids can regress a bit when dealing with situations like this. Their behavior may change, or they may have trouble with bedwetting and even bathroom accidents during the day. As long as you are aware that these changes are related to the trauma, it helps to handle it. Don't take it personally, and try to be patient with them." She handed me her card. "Please let us know if you are struggling or need any help. That's what we're here for."

I took the card and thanked her. At this point, I could only hope that the boys would be with me long enough that I could help them through it all.

I was emotionally exhausted by the time we got home. Charlie and Braden exploded into the house. My kids were there to greet them, and it was smiles and laughter all around. I sank down on the couch and watched as all the children went off to play, obviously happy to be together.

This felt safe. Charlie and Braden were secure and protected here in our home. I was able to relax a bit for the first time, knowing that they were okay. Still, in the back of my mind, the thought nagged at me that Josh would eventually come to pick them up. I tried not to think about it.

Somehow, we all managed to keep eating and taking showers and reading stories to the kids. I don't know what I would have done if Jessica hadn't been there. With Kirk gone, I felt totally adrift in the unknown. When I had talked to him the night before and told him Josh's story, he began to share my certainty that Josh was involved in harming Susan. I needed him here with me to buoy me up and support me through it all.

Kiirsi and I talked again, and I spent the rest of the evening reaching out to those who had expressed concern for Susan. Her church leaders and friends and family, we all wanted to stay connected to each other, as if that somehow would help us to connect to her. To find her.

We started working on getting the kids to bed. Charlie was hard to settle down, being in a different house, but Braden was especially upset. He seemed to fear bedtime. With the other children just drifting off, Braden screamed and thrashed, throwing a monster-sized temper tantrum.

Jes tried everything to calm him while I took care of the other kids. Finally, she took him into the garage and sat in the car with him so the others could sleep. It took two hours for him to finally calm down and fall asleep. Jes carried him inside and laid him down. Even after Jessica went off to bed, I couldn't calm my mind down enough to go to sleep. It was around one a.m. when I crawled under my blankets, drained beyond capacity, and forced my eyes to close.

Josh had never come to pick up the boys. It was a relief. I wanted them to stay longer. I wished they could stay forever.

CHAPTER SEVEN

The next morning started with a knock on the door. I opened it, expecting a neighbor or even the police. Instead, I was met with a camera aimed at me and a microphone thrust in my face.

"Have you heard anything from Susan?"

"Do you suspect your brother?"

"Um . . ." I answered, stupidly.

Questions followed, one on top of the other. I looked over the reporter's head to see other news vans lining up along the curb.

"Um, no comment." I closed the door and rested my forehead against the smooth surface, drawing deep breaths.

From then on, the ringing of the phone and the doorbell were a constant punctuation to the stress of the day. I hid in my house, away from the cameras and questions. I ignored the phone whenever I didn't recognize the number, and I prayed for this storm to pass. For this whole, hairy nightmare to disappear.

Jes was my buffer. She answered the door and refused interviews on my behalf.

When Kiirsi called and told me about a Facebook page she had started, I was torn. I wanted to help in any possible way, but everything was too raw, too emotional, and I felt it my most important duty to keep the boys safe. That meant focusing on them, not the media. But her efforts then, and ever since, were herculean. I watched her constant work on Susan's behalf in awe.

And all this time, we waited for Josh. He didn't call or come by, even though Maxwell told me that he hadn't been charged or arrested and had left late the night before. I waited on tenterhooks. When was he going to show up to take the boys away? It was the worst possible feeling, knowing there was nothing I could do about it.

The day was agonizingly slow, but finally, *finally*, it was time to go pick up Kirk from the airport. I left the kids with Jessica.

"If Josh calls or shows up, call me immediately." I wanted to tell her not to let the boys go. But what would she be able to do?

I kept my head down on the way to the car, and I almost laughed as I left the reporters behind me. But the relief couldn't last long. On the way to the airport, I found myself pushing the edges of the speed limit the whole way. Every cell in my body was straining to get to Kirk, to see his face, to feel his arms around me.

He was waiting for me in the pick-up zone, and I had never seen anything more welcome. He quickly loaded his bags into the van, and I got out and walked around to the sidewalk. He opened his arms, and I collapsed against his chest, all the emotion of the past few days bubbling out through my eyes and watering his shirt. He just held me and rubbed my back for a moment until I could calm down long enough to get back in the car. Kirk drove, and I leaned my head back against the headrest, drinking in the sight of him.

"So what's the status?" he asked.

"They didn't charge Josh with anything, and he left the police station late last night, but I haven't heard from him. They confiscated his car and his cell phone, so I can't reach him. I have no idea where he is."

I could see the wheels turning as he mulled over this information. "And how are the boys doing with all of this?"

"Braden's had a hard time sleeping, but, other than that, they're fine. They haven't asked for Susan at all, but then again, they're so comfortable at our house, I guess that's not that odd. Still, I keep wondering if Josh told them not to talk about her. I really don't know."

Kirk put his hand on my knee, and we talked about how to proceed with the kids.

"Honey, I just want them to stay with us."

"Me, too. But if he comes to pick them up, what can we do?" Kirk asked. I shook my head. I knew he was right. It was what I had been thinking earlier, but I still hated the thought.

When Kirk walked in the door, we were met with mayhem. Garrin was already in bed, but the other children jumped and climbed all over Kirk. He laughed and hugged each one of our children in turn, making sure to include Charlie and Braden. The boys giggled as Uncle Kirk swung them around and blew ticklish raspberries on their cheeks. I thought about Josh's cold behavior earlier, how he had allowed the boys to play near broken glass, and the lack of affection he had shown before leaving the house. It was a stark contrast.

I had originally planned to spend Wednesday night with Susan, Mom, Lori, Jessica, and my oldest daughter, Kristen, at a special Christmas performance of Michael McLean's The Forgotten Carols. We had all been looking forward to a girl's night out, especially Susan. Throughout the day, I had wondered if I should still go now that Susan was missing. I encouraged Mom and the rest of the girls to go and enjoy it, but I just wanted to be there to spend time with Kirk and wait to hear back from Josh or the police.

Mom came upstairs when Kirk got home and told me that she wanted to stay home, too. "Josh called and said he was going to pick up the boys tonight. I'm going to stay here. I need to help him pick up his van from the police and return the rental car. I need to be there for him. He must be so worried."

I couldn't answer. A thick lump formed in my throat. Mom's faith in Josh was hard to stomach. Couldn't she see through the lies? I had the urge to run and hide the boys. But what could I do?

We waited for hours, through the afternoon and evening. Kirk went to bed early, exhausted from his trip. And as it got later and later, I started to relax. It appeared we'd have Charlie and Braden at least one more night. We had just started getting all the kids ready for bed—pajamas on, teeth brushed, and stories read—when Josh came to the door.

The reporters had left for the day, and the night was quiet and bitterly cold. Josh brought the chill of winter inside with him when I opened the door.

At least the boys were glad to see him.

"Daddy," Charlie said. He came up to give Josh a hug, and Braden followed behind.

Still, it was nothing like the reunion I'd seen with Kirk and our kids. Josh acknowledged them with a forced, baby-like greeting.

"Charlie, Braden. Have you been having fun?" His voice was overly sweet, and the cheerfulness was about as genuine as Velveeta. After only a minute or two talking to them, he sat down on the stairs, his shoulders slumped and his face gloomy. The kids were all wide awake now. They started running around and goofing off again, thrilled at the short bedtime reprieve.

Josh looked at us and sighed, his face grave. "I guess I'm going to need to get the kids into counseling to deal with the loss of their mother."

Jes and I looked at each other, shocked. It had been two days. How had his mind jumped there already unless he knew something? If it had been two months of trying everything to find Susan, then maybe that would have made sense. But two days? I don't know if Mom was aware of our negative reaction, but she changed the subject.

"We thought we'd see you last night."

"Well, I got away from the police station really late. They still have my car, so I had to take a cab to get the rental at the airport. By the time I was done, it was midnight." He kept glancing around, his eyes shifting from his feet to the door to his hands. Never looking any of us in the eye. "I drove by, but everyone was asleep, and I didn't want to bother you."

That was ridiculous. Since when did Josh care enough to not want to bother someone else? Besides, I had been up until at least one that night, with the lights on, clearly visible from the street through the second story window.

"So where did you go?" I asked, knowing full well the police had still been searching his house.

"I just drove. I kept driving and driving around, you know." He shifted in his seat. For someone who liked to dominate the conversation as much as Josh usually did, he had been remarkably quiet since all this had happened.

"What did the police say?" Mom asked.

"Oh, they wanted to know about Susan, and where she was and stuff." He looked down at the carpet, and I clenched my fists together in my lap. I wasn't buying the expression of concern. "So, I just came to get the boys."

"But where are you going? Can you get back in your house yet?" I asked.

"Yes, but media is camping out all over my street."

It was true. I'd seen the news, and his house was far more inundated than mine.

"So, you'd better stay here," Mom offered. My breath caught in my throat, and I held perfectly still.

She wanted him to stay here? In my house? I opened my mouth, ready to argue. But Braden toddled up and held his arms out, asking for me to hold him. All the air went out of my argument. I nodded.

"Um, yeah. Okay. The boys are all settled in here anyway."

And that was what mattered, I knew.

Keep them safe. I could almost hear Susan's voice in my ear.

Josh agreed and took his coat off. I went downstairs to get the blow-up mattress.

All night, I tossed and turned. Kirk was a solid, comforting presence beside me, but my mind wouldn't rest. Braden was fussing a lot; I could hear Josh trying to deal with him downstairs. At one point, he even came in with Braden. He was barely visible in the moonlight that leaked through the blinds.

"I can't get him to calm down. Can you take him?"

I was half asleep, but I sat up immediately, reaching out for Braden. But as quickly as he had come in, he changed his mind.

"Never mind," he sighed, then went back out, closing the door.

It was a long, long night.

The next morning, he was off again, running errands or something—he didn't say what. We tried to have a normal morning with the kids, but the throngs of reporters camping outside were a stark reminder how not-normal things were. The news vans were back, parked up and down the street. The cameramen set up their equipment on the sidewalk, but it was so cold that the people all huddled inside their vehicles. With any movement in or out of our house, they would all jump out of their cars and dash to the cameras.

When I heard a car pull up, I went to the window and peeked through the blinds.

It was Josh, still driving the rental car. My heart sank. Maybe this was the time he would take the boys and leave. I watched him open the car door and get out, a stocking cap pulled down low over his ears. All the reporters dashed for their equipment. One figure caught my attention. I recognized Chris Jones from channel 2 as he made a beeline for Josh. I covered my mouth, but couldn't look away. It was like watching a train wreck.

Part of me desperately wanted to keep our family crisis private, but I also wondered if the reporter could get some real information out of Josh. They talked for what seemed like a long time, but it was probably only a few minutes. Then Josh headed up the driveway toward the door. I scooted away from the window, out of view from the cameras, and called to Mom.

"Josh is here."

He came in and sat silently in the living room while Mom grabbed her coat. Then they were off, braving the cold and the reporters, to go swap the cars.

Every time he left, it was like the lights had all come back on in the house. And yet, we knew he'd be coming back. . . .

The afternoon flew by, and it was dark when Josh and Mom returned. He went down the few stairs that led to the playroom and greeted the boys, then sat quietly to the side, watching them play. I stared at him over the railing from the kitchen.

Josh's actions and his lack of any real explanation looked extremely suspicious, but as he sat there with his boys, I wanted *so* badly to believe that he was innocent. Josh had many problems, but I truly did not want to believe that he could be a murderer. He was still my brother, and I wanted to give him the benefit of the doubt.

Kiirsi called while Jes and I were throwing together a quick dinner.

"Are you watching the news?" she asked breathlessly.

"No, why? Have they found something?" Her tone set my heart pounding.

"You have to turn on channel 2. They said they are airing an interview with Josh."

I hung up and hurried to my room. I closed the door, then turned on the TV. Josh's interview started, and I recognized the scene I'd witnessed earlier.

Chris Jones was scrupulously polite, but he asked the difficult questions. My heart sunk lower and lower as Josh evaded every answer, not even bothering to come up with solid excuses.

"How are the boys doing?" Chris asked.

"They seem to be doing good," Josh said.

"Yeah, right. Like you know. You hadn't even seen them in days," I whispered under my breath, bitterness choking me.

"How have you been handling all of this? It's got to be hard?" Chris asked.

Josh looked down at his keys in his hand and shuffled a bit. "Yeah, I'm just trying to . . . figure out what I can do. So I don't sit idle."

It was hard to watch. I jumped up from my seat on the side of my bed and paced in front of the TV. Chris continued to grill Josh about his claim to have taken the boys on a camping trip.

"I frequently take the boys on camping trips. Nothing big, just overnight. We have s'mores and stuff."

"So you took them camping. Where did you go?"

"We went . . . down south. To some trails down there."

Chris pressed him. "Like around Moab?"

"No, not that far. We went . . . to the, um, pony express trails." He was really fidgeting and didn't look Chris in the eye. I felt nauseous.

"Are there camp sites at the Pony Express trails?"

"Um . . . yeah, I think . . . a few."

Chris gave him a reprieve from that specific question. It was obvious Josh didn't have a good answer.

"So what time did you leave?"

"I got off to a pretty late start." The hedging continued, and Josh denied having any idea where Susan was. He said she'd gone to bed at a regular time and that he didn't even know where to start looking for her.

Chris finally let Josh escape, and I snapped the TV off. The doubts about Josh's guilt were entirely gone. I knew Josh. If he had information, he would have talked as long and loud as anyone could have stood it. He usually dominated every conversation from a sheer desire to be at the center of attention, especially if he thought it showed off his intelligence.

I knew that if Susan had actually left like he was suggesting, he would have been proclaiming what a rotten deal it was to anyone who would listen. This Josh was a lie.

I walked slowly back down the stairs, my heart heavy under the crushing weight. If Susan was dead, and my heart whispered that she was, then I had a murderer in my house.

CHAPTER EIGHT

Almost immediately, Josh started gathering the boys' things. Panic gripped me as I faced the fact that he was actually taking the boys and leaving. It only took one look at my face for Jes to see what I was feeling. She tried to intervene.

"Why don't you leave the boys with us for a few more days?" she asked. "It'll give you some time to handle everything, and they are doing so well here."

Josh considered it for a moment. I held my breath, hoping he'd see reason. How could he take care of their needs when he'd never been willing to help with the basics like changing diapers or feeding the kids? It had been a source of contention between him and Susan many times. My heart plummeted when he shook his head.

"No. We need to go. I want to go to the candlelight thing tonight, though. Do you have any candles and matches?"

I cringed. It had been Kiirsi's idea to put the vigil together, a show of solidarity and support from Susan's loved ones. It was like rubbing salt into a wound that he wanted to be there.

Luckily, Jessica handled it. She went to the cupboard and found a few random candles and a small box of matches. "That sounds nice," she said as she handed them to Josh. The false sweetness in her voice was obvious to me, but Josh accepted it at face value.

As he loaded the boys' things into the van, I got out their coats and hats. Charlie was feeling a little rambunctious, and it was hard to get him to hold still long enough for me to zip him up, but he finally calmed down. I held his face between my hands and looked into his eyes. I wanted to imprint my love on him, some sort of talisman against any harm that might be ahead. But he started to squirm, eager to be away. I kissed both his cheeks, tickling his ribs at the same time, and he squealed and giggled, then ran to his dad. Braden was quiet and acting a little sleepy. I bundled him up, then scooped him into my arms for a quick squeeze. Josh was waiting, so I handed Braden to him, and they went out to the car. I watched as they drove away, then continued to stare down the street, tears burning the backs of my eyes.

I felt a little guilty about not going to the vigil. After all, it was for the people who loved Susan, and I really did want to be there. But I knew it would be swarming with reporters, and I was not ready to face them yet. So I stayed safe in my house and placated myself by watching it on the news. The family gathered together, Kirk at my side and our children surrounding us.

The news anchor made a few comments before they switched to the video in the park. There were at least fifty people gathered. Some of them, I recognized—Kiirsi, Debbie, and a few other ward members, family and friends I'd met before. They lit their candles, and Kiirsi said a few words. I imagined what the scene would have looked like from the inside. Reporters would be hovering around the outside of the circle, capturing our tears on camera. My heart was there.

There was a flurry of activity when Josh showed up. He evaded all the questions and stood at the outside of the circle with the boys, all three holding candles. I wondered what was going on in his head. The boys appeared to be okay, at least. He didn't stay long, and the reporters followed him back to his car, firing questions at him all the way.

The news camera zoomed in on a picture of Susan that someone was holding. The candlelight lit up her face. My breath caught in my throat, and I leaned against Kirk as the tears poured down my face.

"I can't bear this," I said silently, sending up a prayer to God. "Please help me to bear this. Please bring her home." The camera panned across the crowd, all with similar tears in their eyes, and, I'm sure, similar prayers in their hearts. A reassuring feeling washed over me, a feeling of peace and calm. It didn't take the pain away, but it seemed to say, "I am here. You are not alone and neither is Susan. Be at peace."

I bowed my head under the feeling, and Kirk wrapped his arm around my shoulder. I reached out and pulled my oldest son, Jeffrey, close to me, and Kristen leaned in closer. We pulled the little ones toward us, and I felt stronger for a moment. My family around me and God watching over all. That was what helped me get through that night and every night since.

It was the longest week of my life. Each day was like a year, stretching out before me in an unending line of questions and waiting. We stayed in touch with the police every day and heard a few interesting developments.

Jovanna Owing, the woman in Susan's ward who had been the last to see her, described this story:

She had come by after church to help Susan untangle some yarn. Apparently, it was a particular gift of hers, and Susan had a large pile of yarn that needed help. While Jovanna and Susan had been busy at it in the living room, Josh had made pancakes for them, even being so kind as to serve it to them in the living room. Shortly afterward, Susan had complained of being sleepy—she was so tired, in fact, that she couldn't keep her eyes open. Josh brought a blanket in and tucked it around her. Jovanna commented on how sweet the gesture was. But before long, Susan apologized to Jovanna and went to her room to go to bed.

The story was bizarre. First of all, Josh cooking? That was women's work in his mind, too far beneath him. Add to that the fact that he served them and then brought Susan a blanket. I had never seen Josh do anything like that. He was too self-absorbed. In the end, Susan was so sleepy that she left her friend in the living room and went to bed. I couldn't imagine Susan ever being that rude to a friend unless she truly couldn't help herself. It raised a ton of red flags.

Another disturbing fact also came to light. Detective Maxwell informed us that the rental car Josh had been driving was returned with eight hundred miles on it, and Josh had no explanation as to where he'd been or what he'd been doing. I was dumbfounded. Detective Maxwell shared the sentiment.

Our relationship with the police improved, but, on the other hand, the reporters were becoming a big problem. Susan's disappearance and Josh's suspicious explanation were making headlines, and every paper and TV channel wanted a piece of the story. It felt like they wanted a piece of me, too.

I stopped on the stairs, just out of sight from the front door as I heard Kirk answer it.

"Is Jennifer here?" I heard a reporter ask. "We'd like to get a statement about her brother's interview." It was the same request they'd all had.

"She's not available right now." Kirk was polite but firm. He closed the door, and I walked down the last few stairs to fall into his arms.

He rubbed my back. "They're not going to be satisfied until they hear from you."

"I know." My voice was muffled with my face pressed into his chest. I turned my head to the side and whispered, "I just can't do it."

"I know."

He understood how devastated I was. I hovered most of the time between disbelief and total meltdown. All of my forced calmness from earlier in the week had evaporated under the strain, and I was incapacitated. Every day that went by—every hour or minute, for that matter—made it less likely that Susan would come home alive and well. And now the boys were gone, too. I could hardly talk honestly to some members of my family, let alone stand in front of cameras and speak the words out loud.

Finally, we decided that Kirk would speak on behalf of our family. He was as distraught as the rest of the family, but he bravely pulled himself together and prepared to represent us. We agonized for hours and hours over the wording of the statement. There was a battle raging in us between sharing our suspicions and presenting a solid family unit. In the end, we knew it wasn't time to go public with our suspicion of Josh. We kept it supportive and neutral. A press conference was arranged for Saturday at the same park where the vigil had been held.

On Saturday morning, we went to Susan's church for a short meeting during which we began a period of fasting and prayer. Her ward members—I'd stopped thinking of them as Josh's ward—and our family and friends were all gathered, and her bishop spoke about the concepts of faith and fasting.

I had found in the past that fasting and prayer, when combined, could facilitate miracles. It seemed the act of denying the body for a short time allowed the spirit to come forward and take the reins, making inspiration that much more accessible. It was a concept that I believed in deeply, and it felt good to be doing something, however small.

After the meeting, we drove to the park for the press conference. As we pulled into the parking lot, I was overwhelmed by how many people were there. I had originally planned on standing beside Kirk during his statement, but there was no way I was going to get out of that car.

"Stay with me, kids," I told them. Kirk looked over, and I shook my head. He understood and left us in the car. I watched him walk toward the cameras and was flooded with gratitude that he would do this. It almost felt like I was sending him to the firing squad. I stayed in the car but watched as he read his statement. As soon as he finished, hands shot in the air, and the clamor of too many people speaking at once carried easily to my ears. His expression stayed calm and patient, and, from what I could tell, he handled it gracefully.

The kids all watched from the backseat. To them, it was cool to see their dad so sought after by the media.

This week had been a surreal experience for them, too: part worry, part interest. Jeffrey and Kristen understood much more of what was going on, and Kristen was especially upset. I had spent a lot of time comforting her since Susan was her favorite aunt. We spent long periods of time in the rocking chair in my bedroom, rocking and crying together. Jeffrey was upset, too, but he had reacted differently. He had started to regress into more difficult behaviors, lashing out in anger with his siblings. His pain was palpable, but I knew it would take some time. I tried to be patient with him. Besides, I had no room to absorb his fears and anger. My own heart was too full of the same.

Jason, Alex, and Abigail were more like echoes, responding to my worry and distress more than feeling it all themselves. They were simply too young to get the gravity of the situation. As far as I was concerned, that was for the best.

Kirk finished with the reporters, though they would have kept him all day if he'd allowed it. By the time we got home, we were all numb, but we dragged ourselves back out that night to put up flyers about Susan all over businesses in our area. We knew there were many, many others who were doing the same all over the state. I felt them with us, their prayers and strength buoying us up.

KIRK'S FIRST STATEMENT TO THE MEDIA

It is hard to know how to start a discussion like this. There are so many emotions and so few facts. Forgive me, as this is very difficult.

We love and miss Susan so much. We are still hoping and praying that Susan will return to us. We feel a unity in this hope, as a family and as a community.

We are so grateful for the love and support and help we are receiving.

Thank you to the police who jumped right in even before we were able to get Susan classified as a missing person, and have guided us through this whole process. They have been very kind and helpful. Their diligence has been appreciated more than they can know.

Thank you to all of our friends and neighbors and even people we don't know, who have joined together on Susan's behalf. The outpouring of love and support has been wonderful, and we are hopeful that support will continue until we find Susan.

Thank you to the media for sharing our situation and keeping this in front of people so that the awareness is as high as possible.

Not having experienced anything like this, it's been very difficult to know what to say and whom to talk to. We want to be as open as possible, and at the same time keep some semblance of normalcy in the day-to-day lives of our children and family.

As a part of our family, her disappearance has left us in shock. You cannot know the heartache her family is feeling at this time.

Our primary concern at this time is finding Susan. Finding her, and returning her to her husband and children, finding her for the sake of her parents, just having her home. We continue to have hope that she will be returned to us safely.

Susan, we love you and miss you and are working and praying for your safe return.

Again, thank you, everybody. Please do not let up in all your efforts.

CHAPTER NINE

From that point on, Kirk was constantly talking to the media. What had started as a local story had caught the attention of the nation, and we were inundated with calls and visits to the house even more than before. Kirk handled it all with as much grace and patience as anyone could have asked for. It was our hope that getting the story out there to a wider audience would help in spreading the word. Maybe someone would hear about Susan and contact the police with a crucial piece of information. Aside from our constant prayers, it was the only thing we could do.

In order to accommodate the differing time zones, Kirk would often be giving interviews as early as 4:30 in the morning or late into the night. We were all exhausted and drained beyond belief.

The tension was so thick in our house that you could taste it. It soured any food or drink we consumed and tainted even the air.

Finally, Jes had had enough. "Let's play cards," she suggested to Jeffrey and Kristen. "Go get your mom and grandma and see if they want to play."

The kids came into the living room to invite us in.

"Not right now." I peeked through the blinds again. The line of news vans in front of our house stretched down the block, and camera tripods were set up along the sidewalk. It felt like a firing squad.

Jes heard my refusal and came to stand next to me.

"Come on, Jenny. Let's try to keep our minds off it all. At least for the kids' sakes."

I couldn't just walk away, though. Not with them all out there. "What about you, Terri?"

Mom glanced at me and shook her head.

"Hey, Jason," Jes called. "Can you open the garage door?"

"What?" I turned to her.

"Let's see what happens?" She had a mischievous glint in her eye that reminded me of the days before this nightmare had started. Jes twitched the blinds to the side, ever so slightly. Mom came to stand beside us as we watched the reporters catch sight of the garage door opening. They all dashed out of their cars and ran for their equipment.

Jes giggled, and I couldn't help my answering smile.

The line of journalists held, their cameras and attention focused with laser-like intensity on my garage. Jes let them hold that pose for a few minutes before calling to Jason again. "Now close it again, Jason."

I heard the low hum of the door closing, but I wouldn't have needed the sound to tell me what had happened. I could see it in their faces, our watchers on the sidewalk. They hung out for another minute and then scuttled back to the warmth of their vans. I couldn't restrain the laugh that burst out. Mom covered her mouth, but her own laughter escaped through her fingers.

"That's mean, Jes," I said with a grin.

"Funny, too. Let's do it again."

And from then on, Jes was newly assigned the job of court jester. She kept us all laughing. It was the only thing that gave us the mildest moment of reprieve in the otherwise horrible miasma of fear and worry. Entertaining us with everything from card games to jokes to innocent tricks on the media like the garage door feint, she was a single bright spot in the darkest of nights.

In private, we discussed the certainty that Josh would soon be arrested for Susan's kidnapping or murder. His story was ridiculous and everyone knew it. As more pieces of information came out, that idea solidified even more. When talking to Jes or to Kirk's family, we shared our feelings freely, but with my family, I kept things to myself. It was too tense to discuss things openly, and it was pointless anyway. We expected the police to be coming after him at any time.

My youngest siblings, Michael and Alina, arrived from Washington on Saturday night, and they stayed with Josh, ostensibly to help him out with the kids and the house. Since Mom didn't have a car, Michael and Alina came to visit her at our house during the first few days. And whenever she had a ride, she went to Josh's house. She wanted to support him and be with her youngest children, whom she didn't get to see often.

For me, it was hard to be there. The house was so empty without Susan's buoyant personality. I found myself staring vacantly around at the rooms that suddenly were so foreign. Maybe if I pressed my face against the wall, I would be able to see what it had seen when Josh had . . .

I caught myself. Had I said any of that out loud? I was growing increasingly worn down by keeping my disgust and suspicion to myself. I swallowed the lump in my throat and focused on my siblings. No one was going to let information slip if they knew what I really thought had happened.

But I didn't have much longer to keep up the front. Late Tuesday night, now a full week after Susan had first disappeared, Kirk did an interview for Good Morning America. He was so tired that it was hard to keep his thoughts straight.

At one point, he was asked, "So, what comes next?" referring to the search for Susan.

Without realizing what he was doing, Kirk gave the answer that we always discussed in private. "We expect that Josh will be arrested in the next week or so," he said. He didn't even realize what he'd said. He finished the interview and fell into bed for a few short hours of sleep. It wasn't until the interview aired early the next morning that everything went wild. The media got hold of that piece of information, and just like that, it was everywhere. The police called us, demanding to know what piece of information we had that made us believe that. We backpedaled frantically with them, and they soon realized we weren't hiding anything, only tired.

But now my family knew where we really stood. I waited for the backlash, but they didn't say anything much at that point. I soon found out how far they were willing to go to keep me out of the loop from then on. I didn't know it then, but I can see now that the rift between Mom and I started at the same time.

On Friday, Josh left for Washington, taking the boys with him. I had no idea he was gone. I called that day to ask how things were going, and Alina answered the phone. She told me everyone was hanging in there, chatted for a minute, and we hung up. She never mentioned that Josh was leaving. That continued on all through Friday and Saturday, with Alina and Michael covering up the fact that Josh and the boys were gone.

The questions from reporters tipped us off.

"Is it true that Josh has left the state and gone to Washington with the boys?" Kirk was asked. "Um . . . I hadn't heard that," he answered, then tried to move on to other topics. He told me later about the question, and I shook it off as false. But when multiple reporters all asked the same question, I was breathless with panic.

We tried to call anyone who could tell us what was going on, starting with Josh. He wouldn't answer our calls. Michael and Alina were the same. I knew that he hadn't been charged with a crime, so he was technically free to do whatever he wanted. That was no consolation. How could the police continue to make any progress on the case with him gone? It was certainly not the act of a grieving, worried husband. I could just imagine his excuse. "Oh sure, my wife has been missing for less than two weeks, so I'm going on vacation." My gut twisted with anger and bitterness thinking of his selfishness.

And the boys would be so far away. I could barely stand to think about it. I couldn't think of anything else.

Kiirsi's husband, John Hellewell, had stayed friendly with Josh with the same agenda in place of trying to get information out of him, and he was the one that finally confirmed the rumor. He called

Josh's cell phone on Sunday, and Josh answered. He told John that he was already in Washington with my dad. John was kind when he broke the news to us, but how could he ease that blow?

I was devastated. If I had any legal recourse, I would have been on the first flight out to go and get the boys. But I was helpless, powerless to keep them safe.

All through the rest of that frigid December, we were on pins and needles. We celebrated Christmas halfheartedly, attempting to make it something special for our children, but unable to find the spirit in the season. Instead of Christmas lights, we hung up fliers with Susan's picture anywhere we could get permission. And instead of pageants or plays, we went to candlelight vigils where we would pray for her safe return, or at least for information that would lead to closure.

And we thought about the boys. As soon as we realized Susan was missing, I had started hoping to adopt the boys, and the idea wouldn't leave me alone. They were so far away, and every cell of my body screamed with a motherly instinct to protect them, to wrap them in the warmth of a family that cared for them and would do anything to keep them safe.

They fit so perfectly in our family, were so well loved, and I knew that Josh wasn't fit to raise them. Even if an observer could somehow overlook the sickening thought of what may have happened to Susan, they would have never seen Josh as a good father. He was self-centered, lazy, and completely oblivious to the needs of another person. Now that he was staying with my dad, the situation would be that much worse. My childhood had taught me that lesson only too well. Charlie and Braden needed a home where their needs would be met and where they wouldn't be fed the slop of conspiracies and delusions that ruled both my dad and Josh.

As the weeks went by, the absence of the boys leeched all the color from the world around me. Over Christmas break, my Uncle Jim, Jessica's dad, came by for a visit. We chatted for a while, though I hardly know what I said, then I left the room to give him some time with his daughter. I was sitting on the stairs, lost in thought, when he came up and sat down next to me.

"How are you doing, Jenny?" he asked, bumping me gently with his shoulder.

"Not too good, actually." My eyes immediately swam with tears. Would I ever stop crying?

He probed a bit, and I couldn't keep my fears to myself. All my worry about the boys came to the surface forcefully and spilled out. I told him how sick I was about the influence the boys would be under.

"They are going to be poisoned and twisted living in that house." I could picture it all too clearly—all the garbage I had lived with growing up would be inflicted on the boys with no one to insulate them the way my mother had insulated me. My stomach was constantly churning as I imagined their environment.

Jim put his hand on my shoulder and looked at me with great compassion. "You know, in the scriptures there are instances where generations are also fed the lies of their fathers. There always came a time when the Lord saw fit to step in and bring them the truth." I felt a tiny leap of hope at his words.

"So what do I do?"

"Make plans for the day when you can get them to safety. Do everything you can on your end to get things in readiness. Talk to a lawyer and talk to Susan's parents. Be honest with them, and let them know your hopes for Charlie and Braden." He smiled and bumped me again.

My answering grin surprised me, and I bumped him back. "Thanks, Jim."

I told Kirk about the conversation, and he agreed that it was the right thing to do. On the Sunday after Christmas, when the kids were occupied with a movie, we went up in our room and locked the door, then turned on the speakerphone and called Susan's parents.

Kirk is always so good at being diplomatic. He has a way with words and putting people at ease. I was more than willing to let him start the ball rolling. He kindly inquired after Chuck and Judy and asked how they were doing.

"We got to see the boys over Christmas. Josh brought them over on Christmas Eve, and then again on Christmas Day. The boys didn't want to leave." His voice was husky with emotion. My eyes pricked with tears. I could only imagine what it must be like for Susan's parents, to be longing for her so much. At least they got to see their grandchildren.

We chatted for a few more minutes, then Kirk saw an opportunity to broach the subject.

"Well, Chuck, as Jenny and I see it, there are only two safe places for the boys right now: your place or ours. We are disgusted with the fact that Josh has them in that environment. Susan would never have wanted them to stay in that house." He went on to describe our worries about the impact that living with Josh and my dad would have.

"Yeah, that's the way Judy and I see it, too." In that brief statement, we were no longer Them and Us. We became a unit called We. We were the safety zone. We continued on with the conversation, discussing the need for attorneys and setting things up so that as soon as Josh was arrested—which we still believed would be any day—we would be ready to legally swoop in and carry the boys off to safety.

From that point forward, we were on the phone with the Coxes nearly every day, discussing plans for the future and checking in with any updates either of us might have. Josh had let the boys visit Chuck and Judy one more time, but then he told them he wouldn't be bringing the boys by because he had some "stuff to do." That stuff turned out to be him coming back to Utah to pack up his house and move it all to Washington.

"I talked to him about us getting back Susan's deacon's bench," Chuck said on the phone one day. "Could you pick it up? I don't expect that he'll ever put the effort into getting any of it to us. I'd rather you take it to your house, and we'll come down and get it."

I agreed immediately. Chuck asked for a few other things—a big box of photos and memorabilia from Susan's childhood, and a couple of gifts that they'd recently sent. All of it was personal between Susan and her parents.

When Josh got back in town, he had Michael with him to help. He'd left the boys with my dad. If I had needed any other sign that he was an unfit father, that would have been it. My dad alone with those two little ones? No good parent would have allowed it.

Kirk and Mom and I went over to help them pack and to get the items Chuck had requested. We spent a couple of hours that first evening. In another circumstance, I may have enjoyed the time with Michael. I had seen him infrequently in recent years, and part of me longed to go back to the relationship we'd had when he and Alina were my sweet, youngest siblings, and I was their friend and protector. But with Kirk's accidental comment to the reporter, an invisible line had been drawn between us. I was on one side of it, and my dad and all my siblings were on the other.

We worked alongside each other, but we didn't say much. As I was packing, I tried to glean any type of information that I could from Josh. I guess I was hoping that I'd stumble across a key piece of evidence while we packed, but I had no such luck.

Jason Randall was Josh and Susan's home teacher. He took his assignment of fellowship through the church seriously and was there helping us pack. As it got late and he mentioned the need to leave, I figured the time had come for me to bring up the items that Chuck had requested. I hoped I'd get a better reaction with a witness nearby.

"Jason, before you leave, could you help me load a few things in my car? We need to get Susan's bench and that box of pictures over there and . . ."

Josh jumped in. "No, no. We have to talk about this later."

"Why? I thought you already talked to Chuck about this. Don't you want to give him back Susan's stuff?" He hesitated for a minute. "I don't understand the problem," I prodded.

Jason stood there, looking confused and uncomfortable. "Who's Chuck?" he asked.

"Susan's dad."

"We'll talk about this later." Josh wasn't going to budge. I could tell Jason felt bad about the situation, but he excused himself and left. We all called our thanks after him, but then my attention went back to Josh.

"Why don't you let me take her photos and stuff for Chuck. I can scan them for you and give you a copy of everything. That way we can have photos for the big media blitz we have coming up."

"No. I'm not going to give them up. Chuck isn't the only one who cared about Susan."

The hypocrisy was too much. Josh hadn't cared about her or anyone else in years. "Fine. Then I'm calling Chuck, and you can talk to him and tell him why you refuse to let him have any of his daughter's personal things." I got my cell phone out and dialed Chuck's number. "Hi, Chuck. I'm at the house, trying to get those things you requested, but Josh refuses to let me take them. I'm going to let him talk to you and tell you why."

Josh was suddenly calm and reasonable-sounding as he took the phone. "No, I don't want to keep them from you. I just want to have a chance to scan them so I can have a copy." He got off the phone.

"That was totally uncalled for. You didn't have to bring that up in front of Jason and Chuck," he muttered. "It was really inappropriate. And the police told me not to give everything away."

What? "Surely they didn't mean that Susan's parents couldn't have her pictures and gifts back."

Finally, he agreed that I could take the bench and the presents, but he wouldn't relent on the photo albums and box of pictures. We took them out the car, and when we came back in, he was still going on about the situation.

"I've been told not talk about certain things, okay?" he said. Kirk and I just looked at each other. What did that have to do with anything? I'd had it.

"Sure, Josh, don't say anything. Just hide behind your lawyers and leave the police to figure out what happened to Susan with no help from you."

Michael jumped on that. "You want to deny him his rights as an American?"

"This has nothing to do with the American Way," I yelled. "This has to do with the fact that we are his family, and he's not telling us anything about what happened!"

"Everyone just needs to stop giving him the third degree," Michael shot back. "You, the police, Dad, everyone."

Kirk jumped up and stepped between us. "That's enough. This isn't helping anything. Let's go." I stared at my family, all lined up together facing me. I wasn't going to get anywhere with them like this.

Josh repeated his earlier comment. "You're not the only one who cared about Susan."

That was all we could take. We left.

All the way home, I replayed the argument, thinking of stinging retorts that I should have said. As we pulled in the driveway, Kirk turned off the car, and we sat for a minute in silence.

"Did you notice how he kept saying he 'cared' about Susan? In the past tense?"

It was true. I hadn't noticed at the time, but that's exactly what he'd said. Another hot wave of rage boiled through me. If this had been any other happy couple, if I'd been the one to die or go missing, it would be reasonable and even expected that the husband would keep all his wife's personal belongings. But this wasn't a usual couple. He was just acting. What I'd said earlier was true. He hadn't cared about her for years

CHAPTER TEN

As frustrated as I was, I remained calm, at least on the outside. Inside, I was a boiling kettle of rage. But, other than the one slipup, I kept my mask firmly in place when it came to my family.

It was mid-January when the idea first occurred to me, terrifying as it was.

I needed to confront Josh.

He had officially moved to Washington a week earlier, and I could think of nothing else but Charlie and Braden, so far away. When Kirk got a work contract that would require him to go to Washington, I knew I needed to go with him.

It had been more than a month since Susan had gone missing, and I longed for knowledge of what had happened to her with every breath. The police had failed to get a confession out of Josh. Detective Maxwell had said he thought if he'd had one more interview with Josh that he could have broken him. But Mom and Michael had told Josh to get a lawyer, and he had cancelled his last appointment with Maxwell. So here we were, still at square one with no idea where Susan was, and now Josh was out of the immediate grasp of West Valley's police department. How were we going to proceed?

I wanted that information, and I wanted it now. But I wasn't going to do anything to jeopardize the investigation. I needed to talk to someone. Jessica was still staying with me. I called her into my bedroom, where we settled into our familiar places. So many times over the last month, we had come in here to discuss the horrifying worries that ate us all up inside. Behind my closed door, we could voice our darkest fears without Mom or the kids overhearing.

Jessica reclined on the bed, and I sat in the rocking chair. "What's up?" she asked.

"You know how Kirk is going to Washington next week? I think that I need to go up there with him. I need to confront Josh." I watched the idea sink in, watched her expression change from interest to shock to worry.

"Wow, Jenny. What are you going to . . . are you going to be okay with that?" She sat up and folded her arms tightly to her body in a protective way. The gesture reflected the way I was feeling so perfectly; it was like she was a mirror of me.

"I don't know. But I can't just sit here, waiting. It feels like every day that goes by without us knowing . . . I need to know." The constant ache of worry in my stomach intensified, underscoring my words.

Jessica's eyes instantly filled with tears. She loved Susan, too. "I understand. But that house, it's an evil place. Your dad scares me. It's unstable. I don't want anything to happen to you."

It was such an accurate description of my father's house that a cold chill washed down my spine, leaving a sick tingle in its wake. The thought wouldn't leave me alone, though. It was that same voice I'd heard warn me away from yelling at Josh on the day Susan had disappeared, and the same voice that had told me something had happened to Susan long before I'd heard Josh's ridiculous story. I just *knew* I had to do this.

"I know, Jes, but this isn't about me. It's about Susan. I'm only worried about compromising the investigation."

"Well, I'm more worried about you." She clenched her jaw, concern etched in every line of her face.

We lapsed into silence, the only sound the slow, rhythmic creaking of my rocking chair. Up until now, I had played the part of the dutiful, supportive sister. Even though the media had got wind of my suspicion, I had never confronted Josh about Susan. To his face, I was his concerned older sister, only wanting the best for him and the boys. I had been too afraid of him running. Well, it was too late. He had done exactly that. What more could I lose?

I stopped rocking. "I think I need to talk to Maxwell and make sure it's not going to cause any problems. Then if he says it's okay, I'm going to do it."

Jessica pursed her lips and looked down. She absently smoothed the blanket in long strokes, her mind far away. I started to rock again and waited. After a few minutes, she looked back up at me. Her eyes were resolved.

"Jenny, you know that I will always support you. If that is what needs to happen, then that's what needs to happen. I can stay with the kids."

That was all it took to bring the tears back to my eyes. They were always so close anyway. Jessica's support was a steady foundation under my feet amid all the rocky chaos.

I talked to Kirk about it later that night on the phone. He was out of town working again, and money stress was keeping him tied in knots. It was a brief conversation. Kirk was apprehensive about it but willing to support me even though the cost of the plane ticket would really hurt. He was as anxious as I was to get some information, and he wasn't as afraid as Jessica. After all, he would be there with me. It was a comforting thought to know I wasn't going in there alone.

The next day, I called Maxwell.

I spelled out the idea briefly, and there was silence on his end of the line.

"So, is it okay for me to do that? To confront Josh and ask him point blank about Susan?"

He cleared his throat. "Well, I can't tell you what to do, who to talk to. What to say. It's up to you." It was the same answer I'd heard from him before. He was covering all his legal bases.

"But?" I prompted.

"But between you and me and the fencepost, you are his sister. You know what bugs him. Give him a titty twister if you have to."

I laughed, surprised by his wording. "I guess you're saying that it's okay, then?"

We both chuckled for a minute. Then another idea popped into my head. I asked him the question before I lost my nerve. "Could you guys back me up? Maybe I could wear a wire and you could hear everything Josh says."

There was silence again.

"Maxwell?" I asked after a minute.

"I'm not sure. I'll need to talk to the D.A. I'll call you back tomorrow." There was a new level of interest, maybe even excitement, in his voice.

The idea buzzed in my head for the rest of the day and through the night. I was waiting on pins and needles. I bought my plane ticket for Washington, and I was determined to go regardless of their involvement, but I would be so much more at ease knowing that there would be policemen there to intervene if things got scary.

When the phone rang the next day, displaying Maxwell's number, I snatched it up anxiously.

He jumped in without a greeting. "The D.A. said that since you were the one who approached us, and not the other way around, we are okay to offer support and to record the encounter."

He described the type of wire they were going to have me carry, something that looked like a keychain, and how they would monitor everything.

"Make sure not to tell anyone about this besides your husband," he warned.

"Um . . ." I stammered.

"Who have you told?"

"I talked to my cousin Jessica about it before I even called you. We were trying to decide if it was a good idea or not."

Maxwell grunted. "Well, just don't mention the police backup or the wire to her, and don't tell anyone else."

"Not even the Coxes? We'll be visiting them."

"No, not even the Coxes. Keep it quiet, or the whole thing could blow up in our faces."

I agreed and hung up. I was reeling. Up until this point, the idea had been abstract, but all at once it was real, concrete. I was going into the house with my brother, the man who had most likely killed his wife. My father would be there, and I usually avoided him at all costs. The reality sunk in, and I found myself trembling with nerves. I wasn't exactly afraid Josh would try to harm me, but then again, I really didn't know. The police apparently felt it was important, even dangerous—enough to provide their support. What was I doing?

I sank down on my bed and stared up at the ceiling. Sounds of my children talking downstairs drifted under the door and wafted around me. Was I willing to put myself in danger with all that I had to lose?

"Please, tell me if this is the right thing to do." I whispered the prayer. Instantly, I felt a calm sense of reassurance sweep over me, and my trembling stopped. Tears ran silently down the sides of my face into my hair, and I drew a steadying breath. I felt calmer, more centered.

I could do this.

The next week dragged by, even with all the arrangements that needed to be made and the usual hectic pace of life. Jessica continued to worry, and I felt bad I couldn't tell her about the police support. All she knew was the visit had been okayed by Maxwell. I had a hard time looking at her when she wore that concerned expression. I couldn't reassure her, and her nerves made my own fears escalate.

Kirk left on Sunday night. This trip was business, after all, and we needed the money. I would follow after a few days, and then we'd go over to my dad's house on Friday. With Kirk gone, my worry got worse. My stomach started to ache constantly, and I couldn't sleep. I kept playing imaginary scenes with Josh and my dad over and over again. I pictured Josh getting defensive and angry, yelling at me in denial. Other times, I'd imagine him admitting the whole thing, even bragging about it. I wondered if my dad would throw us out. That sent a new wave of panic through me. What if they wouldn't even let me in the door? It wasn't like we were on the best of terms, after all. Would this all be for nothing?

When it at last came time for me to leave, I had reached the point that I was eager to have it done. I couldn't bear thinking about it anymore. At least the idea hadn't occurred to me weeks and weeks before I could go. The waiting had been torturous enough as it was.

I kissed my kids goodbye, giving them each the charge to be extra good for Jessica. They had no idea what I was going to do, and I was grateful. Mom had gone to stay with her brother for a few days and didn't even know I was leaving. As Jessica drove me to the airport, a small voice in the back of my mind kept asking if I would see them again. I tried to shush that voice, tell it to be quiet and stop being dramatic, but it continued to nag at me.

When I boarded the plane, I couldn't help looking around at all the other passengers with envy. I wondered if they were traveling for work or going on vacations. Some were probably going to see family and friends or were on their way to a romantic getaway. What I wouldn't trade to be one of them, carefree and excited. Instead, I was hurtling at 500 miles per hour toward the most terrifying task I could imagine. The plane ride was too short.

But Kirk was there when I arrived. I melted into his arms and breathed deeply for the first time in days.

"How are you doing?" His eyes searched my face.

"Better now." I cuddled closer against his chest for a brief moment before releasing him. He picked up my bag with one hand and grasped my hand with the other, and we started toward the exit. I studied him as we walked.

"You look tired."

He shrugged. "I haven't been sleeping well. I could hardly concentrate on the class I was teaching. Are you sure we're doing the right thing?"

I considered the question. Yes, I was afraid. More afraid than I'd ever been, but under that fear was . . . what? Peace? That wasn't quite the word. It was a more of a determination, a strong knowledge that what we were doing was right. I let that feeling ground me, and then willed it to travel through me to Kirk.

"Yes. I'm sure."

He glanced at me with a little surprise at the strength of my voice.

"Okay. Let's do it, then."

The next afternoon, after Kirk's class, we drove to the Pierce County Police department. Maxwell and Detective Cook from the

West Valley Police Department met us there and escorted us into a room that was packed with people. The faces were a blur to me. My eyes didn't want to focus. I gripped Kirk's hand harder, and he gave it a reassuring squeeze.

Maxwell introduced the other men in the room, but each name was gone from my mind before he said the next one. I tried to smile and greet people, but I was relieved when the introductions were done and I could sink down into the offered chair.

"So, we've made plans to have support at hand through the entire process. You'll have a couple of unmarked cars right down the street, a surveillance van nearby listening in to the conversation, and a helicopter in the air the entire time."

I was astonished by the scope of the police involvement, but each detail straightened my spine with the reminder that I wasn't doing this alone. I could tell that Kirk was feeling equally relieved. He leaned forward with interest.

"What about the wire?"

"Well, we are still planning on you carrying a small device. It's about the size of a keychain, and you'll just keep it in your pocket. In addition, we've decided to put another wire and a tracking device in the trunk of your car. So if you need to go anywhere, make sure that you take your car."

I'd never even considered the idea that Josh or my dad might try to get me to go somewhere with them. What a relief to have the police taking care of the details.

"Do we need to use any code words to let you know if there is a problem?" Kirk asked.

Maxwell shook his head. "Your code words are 'help' or 'he's got a gun.' Don't make it too complicated. We'll be right there if anything goes wrong."

It was clear cut. Go in, act normal. I needed to get Josh away from everyone, ask him about Susan, and press him for details. If there was danger, tell the police through the wire, and they'd be right there. I got the gist of it; now I just wanted to get it over with.

When we pulled onto my dad's street, my heart was beating so hard I thought it might leap right out. I pressed my hand against my chest, trying to calm it, trying to keep it together. *Just breathe*, I told myself. We drove past two unmarked cars with men sitting in the

73

front seats. Their presence was reassuring, but I was going in there alone.

I looked over at Kirk. His face was grim. No, I was not alone. Kirk was with me, and I knew I had God on my side, too. I reminded myself of the reassurance I'd felt about this before. Everything would be okay. That thought steadied my nerves enough that I could get out of the car and walk toward the front door. For better or worse, I was going in there, and I was going to do everything I could to get Josh to talk.

I raised my hand. It was steady. I knocked on the door.

CHAPTER ELEVEN

John opened the door and was quickly backed up by the rest of the family. There were shocked faces all around, but they invited us in. I was disappointed that my dad was there. I'd hoped he wouldn't be home yet so I could talk to Josh more easily. Even more than that, I had avoided him so well in recent years. Now that I was seeing him face to face, I was cold all over. Old memories of our confrontations came charging in, threatening to send me running back to the car.

I cleared my throat before I could lose my nerve.

"Kirk was here for work, and I decided to come with him so I could visit." The excuses sounded flat in my ears, but they didn't respond skeptically. At least that was a relief. I had brought two big lollipops for the boys. After more than a month away from us, they might have been persuaded to hate or fear me. I had no idea what they'd been told. The treats were offerings to ease the way.

It turned out that they weren't needed. Charlie and Braden were so excited to see us. They jumped on Kirk and me, and we spent a few blissful moments holding them, reassuring ourselves that they were safe and whole. I would have liked to lose myself in playing with my sweet nephews, but the recorder in my pocket weighed a hundred pounds. I was here for a different purpose.

"I hope we aren't interrupting anything," I said, forcing myself to make eye contact with my dad.

"No, we're just making dinner. Why don't you come in and join us?" It was a better reception than I'd expected. We followed them down the hall to the dining room. Kirk and I sat down at the table, and the boys immediately climbed into our laps and demanded our attention. We played with them and listened to their cute little babble about their toys and other childlike matters. My dad went into the kitchen to make dinner while we sat on the couch and read picture books. Being with Charlie and Braden was soothing and encouraging. It was a reminder of why I was here, putting myself through this.

After a while, we went to the table and sat with the rest of the family and made small talk—jobs and our kids and neighbors; they even invited us back for Charlie's birthday party the next day—everything but the most important topic we could have discussed. Not one word was brought up about Susan. Not even by the boys. It was a bizarre contrast. At home, there had been no other topic of conversation for nearly two months. How could they not even mention her?

I excused myself to go to the restroom. I was supposed to text Maxwell with a description of what Josh was wearing so he would be easily identifiable in the event that they needed to come in. That was when I realized that we didn't have any cell service. I remembered my sister complaining about it in the past, but it had never registered that we'd have a problem. Now we couldn't get communication from the police. I thought about talking into the recorder to pass along the information, but what if my voice echoed? The bathroom was right by dining room. My family might have heard me.

When I came back out, I leaned close to Kirk's ear. "We don't have cell service." He got the implication. A couple of minutes later, he started asking Josh about his shirt.

"What is that logo?" Kirk asked. Josh glanced down at his shirt and then launched into a story about where he'd gotten it. He was always willing to talk about himself. So, at least the police had an idea of what he was wearing.

Dinner was ready and we continued the act. I had no idea how to begin digging. I ate my food, knowing that the police were on standby in cars nearby, a helicopter was circling overhead, and a recorder sat in my pocket, all anxiously taking down the information that . . . I was eating a pork chop. My dad and my four siblings all sat around the table, Josh across from me.

Yes, the boys were glad to see us. That was comforting. But that wasn't why we were here.

We finished dinner, and Alina started to clear the dishes. Josh stood up. The time had come. I looked at Kirk and nodded. He understood and gave me a brief nod in return. I lifted Braden off my lap and stood up, moving to Josh's side. I took his arm.

"I wanted to talk to you for a minute. Let's go in the other room." Josh didn't act terribly surprised by the question, but my palms were slick with sweat. I wiped them on my jeans as we walked to the front of the house and went into my dad's music room. Kirk stayed in the family room with the boys and tried to keep everyone else's attention focused on him.

The music room was filled with an electric piano, a guitar, a number of microphones, and some recording equipment. It was cluttered with books and papers covering the desk and the bookshelves. The door was glass and framed by windows on either side. I closed the door behind us and glanced around the room, then forced myself to go forward. Josh leaned against one wall, where he could look out the window and down the hall toward the family room. I sat in the chair at the desk and cleared my throat.

"I've just been worried. I've been hearing rumors. You know, rumors about you that say you're going to be arrested soon."

There was the slightest bit of a flicker, and then Josh turned off the emotion again and was cold and calm.

"Where did you hear those rumors?"

"Oh, from reporters and stuff."

Josh's eyes were blue, but right then they appeared black. Maybe it was a trick of the light, but it looked like they were nothing but pupils, no color at all.

I continued trying soft ways of getting him to talk. Prodding here and there and watching his eyes all the time.

"Please, I'm your sister. Confide in me. I want to believe you. If you would only give me something to go on."

There was no reaction. That first startle was his only hint of emotion.

"Don't make me listen to rumors, tell me your side of the story."

Nothing.

"If you don't give me anything else to go on, you give me no choice. I'm starting to doubt your story. I don't believe you anymore."

"Well, I'm sorry you feel that way."

Michael came down the hall, opened the door and stepped inside. "Are you ready to go pick up the party stuff for tomorrow?" he asked. Had my dad sent him to intervene? I didn't care. I had to keep trying.

"There has to be something more you can tell me. You know something." His dark pupils made him look like a stranger. I rubbed my arms against a sudden chill. "Come on, Josh. I can see it in your eyes."

He pushed away from the wall. "We need to go get the cake," he said, nodding to Michael. It was a convenient excuse, and they left the room without looking back at me. I followed behind them more slowly.

I'd come all this way, endured all the stress and worry and expense for one purpose—to get a confession out of Josh. I couldn't give up now. Josh was standing in the family room near the bathroom door, waiting for Michael to get his coat. I grabbed Josh's arm and half-yanked, half-pushed him into the dark bathroom. Everyone else was still talking, and the boys were playing loudly. It was too much to hope that no one noticed what was going on.

"Josh, let's just cut the crap. Tell me what really happened. Did you actually go camping? What did you do that night?"

Josh tried to squirm away, but I held on tighter to his arm and blocked the door. "My lawyer told me not to talk about it," he said.

"That's crap! I'm your sister. Don't pull that lawyer thing with me. Just tell me what happened. Tell me where her body is. We want to have a funeral and have some closure here. Just tell me where you put her." I half expected him to hit me, but instead there was still no emotion. He didn't respond in anger. He didn't respond at all. He shrugged his arm out of my grasp and pushed past me.

I stayed in the bathroom for a minute and tried to calm my breathing. My heart was racing, and adrenaline was pumping through my limbs, but it started to fade all too soon, leaving only disappointment and shaky weakness in its wake. I heard Josh, John, and Michael leave the house, heard the front door close. I knew that I wasn't going to get any information out of him, but I also knew he was guilty. If someone had accused me of hurting my husband or my children, I would have punched them at the very least and kicked them out of my house or something. His lack of emotion was as telling as a confession to me.

But it wouldn't do any good in a courtroom.

I stepped out of the bathroom and signaled to Kirk with a finger pointing at the ground that I wanted to stay. I had to get some tiny piece of information or this would all be for nothing.

I sat back down at the table, and Alina and my dad were leaning against the counter opposite me.

"It's not going to be long now before there is an arrest." The boys were close by with Kirk, so I tried to keep my wording careful and vague for their sakes.

My dad laughed, short and mirthless. "Well, Jenny, you've always lived in your own reality. You think you know so much more than the rest of us. There's not going to be any arrest." He shook his head disapprovingly. "I think it's time you were going. And don't come back for the party." I felt defeated, but what else could I do?

Kirk and I glanced at each other. It was time to go. We hugged and kissed the boys and said goodbye, then followed my dad toward the front door. The boys were still in the family room, and I desperately hoped they wouldn't be able to hear my next question.

"So, did you help him kill her, or did he just tell you about it afterward?" I asked quietly. He was almost to the front door. He spun around, a lengthy string of profanity spilling out of his mouth. He called me every filthy, vile name imaginable. Alina jumped in.

"Susan is such a b____!" She hesitated for a second, and it hovered in the air as if she'd spoken: *she deserved whatever she got.*

Jennifer Graves and E. G. Clawson

I was stunned. My dad's attack, I expected, but this was from Alina. What could she have against Susan? I could see my dad's disapproval of Alina's tactic.

"This isn't about Susan. This is about you, Jenny, and your mother. This is about the divorce!" he spat out. "You are always taking her side in everything, and I'm always the bad guy, right? I'm always the one in the wrong."

Kirk reached out and took my arm and pulled me along gently, trying to get me out the door. I let him pull me along. How had the topic been changed so fast? I was baffled as to how to keep going for more information. We made it through the door and started toward the car with my dad and Alina following behind us, yelling at us. Alina was simply parroting my dad's complaints about the divorce back at me. It was pathetic and heartbreaking. She was only seven when the divorce began.

We didn't respond. It was over. I was only glad that the boys were still inside so they didn't have to hear this. We got in the car, and my dad hollered after us.

"Never come back here. You're not welcome here again."

Kirk put the car in reverse, and we backed out quickly. By the time we turned out of the neighborhood, it hit me. We'd made it through.

But we hadn't gotten a confession. I cried all the way to the police station. All of the tension that had built up now broke loose, and I started shaking all over.

The police station was just a few blocks away. When we went inside, we were met with cheers. I laughed, but I couldn't stop shaking.

Maxwell grinned at me. "For a minute there, I thought we were going to rumble." We returned the wires, and they took the tracker out of the car. The police had heard everything, but they still had a few questions to clarify. Nothing really useful had been discovered unless it was the lack of emotion on Josh's behalf. That was telling, as far as I was concerned, but I had nothing more to give them.

I was still shaky all the way to the hotel. I called Jes to give her the details of the encounter even though I couldn't share the fact that I'd been wired. She had been waiting anxiously to hear I was okay. She was properly appreciative of how amazing I'd been.

But then I had to call my mother. She was staying with Uncle Jim for the weekend. That's how I'd been able to get away without her knowing I was gone. I knew she would eventually hear it through the grapevine, and I didn't want it to come out that way.

"Hi, Mom. I wanted you to know. I'm in Washington. I went to Dad's house this evening and tried to get Josh to confess." She was obviously in shock.

"Um, ok. How are the kids?" She meant her kids. "Are they upset? Are they ok?"

"Well, Dad was swearing at me at one point, and they'll probably be upset. I'm sure you'll hear about it. But everyone is ok."

Later, Mom asked me outright if I'd been wearing a wire. I guess that my siblings and dad started to put it all together and tried to get her to dig for information. I told her I hadn't, and I only felt a little bad for lying to her. And how ironic that she would dig for information when it might help Josh, but she refused to volunteer any information when it might help the police find Susan.

I didn't get a confession from Josh or my dad that day, but if I hadn't tried, I know I would always have wondered if I could have done more. At the very least, I did gain the confidence of the police. As the months went by, they were much more willing to talk to me and ask me questions.

And the next morning, when we stopped by to visit Chuck and Judy, I was able to hold my head high and have a clear conscience, knowing that I was firmly entrenched on the right side of this case. I had burned my bridges with my family irrevocably, including with my mom to some extent, but from here on out, there would be no more pretending.

PART TWO:

CHOOSING A PATH

"If you are not willing to learn, no one can help you.
If you are determined to learn, no one can stop you."
-Anonymous

CHAPTER TWELVE

I'm not sure how old I was when I first realized that my father wasn't like my friends' dads. When I was a young child, my family seemed normal. It was all I knew. It was as I approached my teen years that the difference became apparent.

To a casual observer, my father was a normal guy. He had some extreme opinions about government and religion, but he held down a job, making a decent living. He spoke well and dressed and acted fairly average. But as the years went by, he descended more and more into a pit of hatred and bitterness that poisoned his marriage and, later, his children.

Dad had a difficult childhood. His parents went through an ugly divorce when he was young that resulted in him and his siblings being caught in a twisted game of tug-of-war. He described to us something that he called his parents' "kidnapping game." He told this story on his website:

> *"In only a matter of months, my dad made a unilateral and secretive decision to separate from my mom. So on a given weekend, he took us to visit his parents while my mom went to spend the weekend with her aunt in Burbank. Unbeknownst to her, my grandparents*

Jennifer Graves and E. G. Clawson

had, prior to that weekend visit, transported their trailer house to Northern California, and parked it in Weed.

When we headed over to see my grandparents and kept going north on Highway 1, something seemed amiss to me, even at seven years old. "Where is Momma?" I asked. Grandma curtly replied, "You're never going to see your mother again." Of course . . . my older brother, my sister, and I were inconsolable.

(www.stevechantry.com)

His mother retaliated later, and that kind of twisted revenge went back and forth for years. My dad grew up with no stability, no ability to control where he would live or which parent he would get to see.

I don't know much about his teenage years, but I do know he was active in the LDS Church. He served a mission for the Church, and later he and my mom were married in the temple. In order to serve a mission or enter the temple, it is necessary to complete worthiness requirements. It is an honor-based system, an interview process. Did my father really believe in what he was doing, or was it all a lie, even then?

Steven and Terrica Powell - 1973

Whatever *his* feelings, my mother was drawn in and fell in love with him. She saw him as an upstanding, religious, "good" young man with big dreams and plans. They were married on June 29, 1973, and settled in to raise a family.

I was born one year and one day later, a healthy seven pound fifteen-and-a-half ounce baby. Mom was ecstatic to be a mother. I know that she was eager to have someone she could love unreservedly, knowing she'd be loved in return. Mom has always been a giver, soft-spoken and caring with a desire to keep the peace and make people happy.

86

Josh was born about a year and half later, in January of 1976, and he was followed one year later by John. There were also two or three miscarriages during that time. Her thyroid wasn't functioning well. With three young children close together and her own poor health, Mom had a lot on her plate.

My dad wasn't actually present much when I was younger. He was busy building a business, he said. He didn't have time to deal with kids and home. Mom was the caretaker, the nurturer, the comforter. My dad was just the guy who told Mom what to do. At least that's how it strikes me now, looking back.

He tried his hand at real estate for a few years. I think he did okay, but it wasn't a stable income. He got a new job selling office furniture to companies and school districts. I used to file invoices for him, and he paid a dollar per hour. There was an old eight track player in the office. I would turn it on and listen to Barbra Streisand, Anne Murray, and Elvis. For an eight-year-old, it was wonderful. I felt grown up—performing an adult task and making money besides.

But his job was hard on Mom. He traveled a lot. When I was young, maybe six or seven, he was traveling for one or two weeks out of every month. The burden of caring for the family fell entirely on Mom's shoulders. But that was woman's work anyway, according to my dad.

Years later, Mom told me that it was in the first year or two that she became aware of my dad's problems. She discovered he was involved with pornography. It was devastating for her. I'm not sure what happened then. Did she confront him? Did he lie to her and smooth things over? I don't know for sure, but nothing changed. He continued to do whatever he wanted.

As a father, he was a boiling teapot and would blow his lid every once in a while. He would be calm for a time, and then all hell would break loose. We never knew which dad we were going to get: the dad who sang songs and told stories or the ranting, terrifying one.

In a supplemental statement during the divorce proceedings, Mom described this behavior:

> *"Steve also had a pronounced habit of ignoring behaviors in the children that bothered him, sometimes over a period of days or weeks. Of course, they [took] his silence as permission; after all, he was*

Jennifer Graves and E. G. Clawson

observing them. Then, suddenly, he would become outraged and react far more violently than was necessary or fair. He would yell at them and call them names, and be too physically rough with them, such as spanking them with too much force and far too long, or shaking them or dragging them around."

This happened frequently with me, Josh, and John. Josh was the most targeted, though. According to Mom, there were years that my dad pointedly attacked Josh on a regular basis, nearly every day. It's true that Josh was a strong-willed boy, but wasn't there any positive way to handle him?

My dad didn't appear interested in trying the softer approach in any area of parenting, though. This was clear in the way that he handled one specific area.

The three of us oldest children all had troubles with wetting the bed. Dad decided he was going to "cure" us of our problems. He would come into my room every morning, early, while I was still sleeping, to check my bed. If it was wet, I would be awakened by my dad picking me up to carry me to the bathroom, where he would fill the tub with icy-cold water.

I remember cowering on the floor while the tub filled, the linoleum cold against my legs. I pulled my damp nightgown down over my legs, trying to stay warm.

"I'm sorry, Daddy. I won't do it again," I whimpered. He ignored me, bending down to shut off the water. I clutched the nightgown more closely as he turned back to face me.

"Please." Then my words were gone, and I cried out as he pulled my nightgown over my head. He tossed it aside, then scooped me up in his arms. The water took my breath away, and I fought him.

But no matter how much I would cry and beg and fight, he wouldn't relent until I had lain down and let the frigid water cover me up to my neck. Only then could I get out. It was horrid and completely ineffective as a cure for bedwetting. I know he did the same thing to my brothers.

Later, I overheard Mom arguing with him. "It's not working. And it's so harsh," she said. But he didn't care what she thought. The torment went on for months.

When I was ten or so, my dad had to travel for business, and for some reason, he took me along with him. I hung out at the hotel while he went on his appointments, then we went out for dinner at a restaurant. It was heaven. Not only was I away from my annoying little brothers, I was doing something grown up with my dad. No matter his faults, I still was a little girl who wanted her father to love her. When we got back to the hotel, we settled in to watch a sitcom on TV. I cuddled down into my bed, relishing the novelty of TV in bed.

But halfway into the show, he changed the channel. A pornographic movie came onto the screen, and I was stunned. I looked over at my dad. Didn't he remember that I was right there? He glanced at me but didn't say anything, just turned his attention back to the screen.

I burrowed down under the covers and covered my head with the pillow. I was sickened at what I had seen in those brief seconds, and the pillow over my head couldn't keep out the sounds that wormed into my ears. Even then, I think I knew that a father is supposed to protect his daughter. I felt exposed and betrayed. Was that appropriate behavior? Especially for a married man? I remember asking myself those questions even then.

Mom was flattened over time by my dad's overbearing and forceful personality. She never compromised her own sense of right and wrong, staying true to her religion. One of the hot topics was paying tithing. Mormons believe in paying ten percent of their income to the Church for building temples, supporting missionaries, and helping the needy. Mom was determined that she would follow this precept. My dad, however, refused. Mom compromised by paying tithing on any money she brought in. As a stay-at-home mom, she didn't have much of an income, yet she tried her best to add to the household funds as much as she could. She babysat, sold small kitchen appliances and herbs, and she faithfully gave ten percent of that little income to the Church. It made her happy to know she was doing her part. She believed that by paying tithing, they would be blessed with the money they needed to support their family.

For a time, the conflict over religion became too much for Mom, and she stopped taking us to church. Her friend, Shareen Campbell, stated:

"For three years, she [Terri] stopped going to church and stopped even having a prayer on their food. Her beliefs didn't change, and she still felt pressure against her."

Obviously, the experiment didn't work. Mom decided that if my dad was going to continue to treat her that way, then she was going back to church and taking her children with her. She has stayed involved ever since.

When my dad was still selling real estate, they were going to be several hundred dollars short one month. Mom talked my dad into paying tithing in advance on the money they would need to get by. A few days later, a cash purchase went through, and they were paid the exact dollar amount they needed. She hoped that would convince my dad to keep going, but he wasn't interested. Mom kept on living the way she believed, hoping my dad would eventually join her. She was consistently disappointed.

Five years after John was born, Mom gave birth to Michael. My early memories of Josh and John paint them as typical obnoxious little brothers, always making noise and running around. But Michael was different. I was eight when he was born, old enough to appreciate his sweet baby smell and tightly curled fists. I had a soft spot in my heart for him. He always seemed more gentle and compassionate. More like Mom. I remember my dad playing the guitar and singing *Edelweiss.* He used to sing to Michael and rock him to sleep. I loved listening to him. He had a beautiful voice. Later, even though religion had become a painful topic, he would still sing LDS hymns. How sad that even this talent would later be perverted and used to sing obsessive love songs about his own daughter-in-law.

During this time, money started becoming more of a hot topic with Dad. He made a sufficient living with his job, and we always had what we needed—maybe thanks to Mom's tithing efforts—but he started to lay on the guilt with her. He made it clear that she was a lesser contributor to the home since she didn't bring in a paycheck. Mom took care of all of us children, the house, the cooking and shopping, and all those other things that kept our family running, but she had very little say about money or about any major decisions. It was strange that my dad couldn't see the disparity between his beliefs that running a household was women's work and that she should also be making money.

He also started to become more and more opposed to the LDS Church. I remember him describing my Uncle Jerry, his brother, as a "fanatical Mormon." He made it sound like Jerry was a backwoods fundamentalist with extreme views and the gun power to protect them. Looking back, I can imagine that anyone who went to church on Sunday and followed the basic tenets of our religion was seen as "a fanatic." When I met Jerry for the first time, I expected him to be a bible-thumping zealot, based on my dad's description. I was surprised to find an average guy, pretty much the same as everyone else I'd ever met who attended any church.

It wasn't that my dad had discovered another religion to be more to his taste or even that he was questioning the doctrines of the Church. It was a bitter hatred that started out small and blossomed into wild-eyed, incomprehensible haranguing that made even other anti-Mormons uncomfortable at times. From that point forward, anything that went wrong in his life or that he perceived to be wrong in the world could be traced back to the Mormons.

Powell family – 1983
From left to right – front: John, Michael, Josh
Back: Jennifer, Terrica, Steven

When Mom was expecting her last child, my little sister Alina, things reached a low point. She was sure he was still involved in pornography, and now she suspected that he was cheating on her whenever he went out of town.

One day, she found a notebook hidden under the bed. It was filled with detailed fantasies about a woman in our ward. She was happily married and completely oblivious to my dad's attraction, I'm sure. But he wrote about being madly in love with her. He obsessed over every word she said and described sexual encounters he daydreamed about. When Mom confronted him about the notebook, he didn't bother to deny it or even feel guilty. He told her that he was in love with this other woman and even went so far as to tell Mom he would become a polygamist (something that is not condoned by my church). He wanted to keep Mom and marry this other woman as well.

Mom was devastated. She fretted over the topic so much that she became ill. My Grandpa John came to visit. He, my grandma, and their two youngest children had recently moved to Mesa, Arizona, and he needed to wrap up some of his business concerns in Spokane. Mom wanted him to stay with us, but my dad was reluctant. It took some talking, but Mom convinced him to let Grandpa stay for a while. She needed the support, but she didn't want to admit to my Grandpa how bad things had become.

Finally, she couldn't keep it a secret anymore. She told him about a notebook she'd found wherein my dad talked about another woman, and how he wanted to marry this other woman. She swore my Grandpa to secrecy, forbidding him to even tell his wife. Grandpa was disgusted. He tried to support her, to help her around the house and offer her counsel, but my dad made that difficult. He wanted his father-in-law gone. Most days, Grandpa would stay away from the house as much as possible, hoping it would lessen the tension and, therefore, the strain on his daughter. He was in a sticky situation. He needed to return home, but he was anxious for Mom's well-being. And Mom desperately wanted him at the birth of her fifth baby, which was imminent. Yet, my dad wanted him out of the house, and my grandma was wondering why he wasn't coming home.

One night, he took Mom out for ice cream, just a short trip to get her away from all the negativity. When they got back, his belongings were on the front lawn. My dad was carrying another armful out the door.

"What are you doing?" Mom called.

"I'm moving your dad out," my dad said, dumping his armful on the ground.

"Oh, no you're not! He is staying here until my baby is born!" Grandpa took Mom inside, and my dad followed. My brothers and I followed behind as the argument moved to the kitchen. It unsettled us to have the adults fighting.

Grandpa continued to try to calm the situation down and reason with my dad, but suddenly, there was my dad, holding a bar stool high over his head, as if he were going to bash Grandpa with it.

Grandpa looked up at the stool and calmly said, "Steve, what are you doing . . . in front of your little kids?"

My dad looked down at us and paused, then put the stool down.

I don't remember the rest, but I know that the sheriff was called, and that they eventually agreed that Grandpa would stay one more night, then leave the house. Mom still wanted him there at the birth, so he went to Pocatello to visit his mother, returning when Mom went into labor.

Powell family – 1986
From left to right – front:
John, Alina, Terrica, Michael
Back: Josh, Jennifer, Steven

The time with Grandpa must have helped Mom gather some resolve. Sometime during that week or two that Grandpa was gone, she confronted my dad. She told him that she wouldn't put up with talk of this other woman anymore. She also made it clear that she and the children would continue going to church. That was non-negotiable, or she would take the children and leave. I can't imagine how hard that was for her. She had never been one to rock the boat, and I know it took courage to lay down the law.

And it helped, at least for a while. At any rate, Mom stayed. For the next couple of years, my dad kept his opinions about the Church and about the government, also a hot topic, mostly to himself, spouting off at home occasionally—but we were used to that.

In 1988, we moved to a new home in Veradale, Washington. It was a bigger, nicer house—a step up, it would seem. But something changed in my dad when we moved. We were no longer around the same neighbors and people that we'd dealt with in the community and at church. We had new people around us, a new ward. My dad took this as his license to lose what few restraints he had previously placed upon himself. He became loud and open with his sentiments, and our lives became much more difficult.

I remember one incident when Mom was gone and my dad was home with us kids. A pair of missionaries came by for a visit. I'm sure they knew that Mom and her kids were active in the Church but my dad wasn't, and they wanted to see if they could reach out to him. I was fourteen at the time, and I knew it was a rule that missionaries should always be with their companions. It provided a level of protection for them, these young men who had left their homes to go share their testimonies with others.

My dad somehow managed to split them up, taking one of them at a time into another room, where he chewed them out violently enough that the leader over that mission had to make it a rule that no missionaries were allowed to visit our home anymore.

I never had friends over. I was too afraid of what my dad might say or do to humiliate me. Any time someone would come over, my dad would verbally attack them or me. He'd put down my religion and find things that would embarrass me. He would criticize me and Mom, making fun of us in front of our guests. As a consequence, I didn't have many friends. I felt uncomfortable putting myself forward in a relationship that would be unequal. I kept mostly to myself, finding comfort in helping Mom with Michael and Alina and playing with my golden retriever, Addie. I had one good friend, Angie, but I hardly ever brought her home.

My Aunt Lori was an exception. Mom babysat her every day when we were little, and she lived close by, so in many ways she was like my sister. But even our extended family couldn't stand to be around my dad too much. Brenda Lissy, a friend of Mom's, described what it was like to try to visit:

> *"Most of the time, Terri and I would discuss our religious beliefs, and it was as if Steve couldn't wait until he could jump in and control the conversation by demoralizing someone, the LDS Church, and/or their beliefs. Any time there was a group of friends and family gathered together, everyone had to make a real conscious effort not to bring up anything to do with religion."*

It wasn't just religion, either. The government, women in general, any sort of law enforcement or authority—all topics were targets.

My home life sometimes felt like a war zone; my father, the general of the opposing army. But I had no idea then the sort of battle lines that would be drawn in the future.

CHAPTER THIRTEEN

Looking back through years of experience, it's easy now to see that there were early signs of Josh's problems. But how could I have ever known then what he would become? He was just my little brother, frequently not a very nice one, but I was a child and then a teenager, not equipped to make judgments or decisions about his well-being. Now, as a parent, I can't help but question—what would have happened if someone had seen those signs for what they were and stepped in to do something about it? Would Susan and the boys be alive today?

Josh was less than two years younger than me, but we were never close. Sometimes, we played together and had fun, but he and John were the friends and co-conspirators, always getting into trouble, always defending one another, and I was just the bossy older sister.

A few incidents stand out in my mind as moments that I knew something wasn't right. Those were the times that it penetrated my youthful brain. I can only imagine there were others that I never knew about or didn't understand.

As the oldest of five children, I often had the responsibility of babysitting my younger siblings while my parents ran errands or went to church meetings. Michael and Alina were easy. They were my sweet younger siblings. I loved to play with them and care for them, and we had a good time together. But Josh and John were a different story. Things would usually start out fine, but whatever game the two older boys would play would quickly turn rough. They would wrestle with each other, but eventually they'd get bored and start teasing me or the little kids. The teasing would escalate until we were truly afraid.

More than once, I took Michael and Alina, who were only three and one or so, and tried to hide from the boys until my parents got home.

I have a vivid memory of barricading myself under the piano one time. I pulled Alina and Michael in after me, wedging the piano bench in front of us like a shield. Josh and John had sticks and were prodding us, trying to get me to relinquish my hold on the piano bench.

"Give me Michael. He wants to play with us," John said.

"Yeah. Alina, too," Josh said. Alina whimpered and curled in closer to me.

"No. Leave us alone. You're just going to be mean again. Get away."

Oh, how I wanted my mother to come home. I always hated it when my parents left. They didn't really understand that it was more than not wanting the bother of babysitting. I never knew what was going to happen. There were no cell phones to call for help when the boys got out of control, and we didn't even have locks on the bedroom doors.

There was no safe haven.

When my parents got home, it was always a relief. I would run to Mom and tell her what had happened. Sometimes the boys would get in trouble, and Dad would take out the belt. Other times, nothing much was done about it. But at least I wasn't afraid anymore. John was probably ten and Josh eleven at the time. They were only children. But even then, they were more than Mom could handle.

Another incident was listed in my parents' divorce papers. I don't think I actually knew about it at the time. We had pet gerbils, and Mom's sister Becky stated:

"A couple of years ago [sometime in 1990] when I was staying there, Alina came up to me (she was about four at the time) and was telling me that there was red on her hand and she didn't like it and was going on and on about it. I finally understood that she was saying Joshua had killed one (or more?) of their gerbils and was making her hold the gerbil and touch the blood. I was appalled . . . Johnny has told me that Josh has killed baby gerbils by throwing them against the side of their cage."

Mom was horrified about his behavior and talked to my dad about it, but he brushed it off and told her that she didn't understand the sense of humor of a teenage boy. It was obviously disturbing and should have been a sign of trouble to come, but it wasn't taken seriously.

One of the most troubling memories from my childhood started out as a happy time. My dad had to travel on yet another business trip for work, but this time our family got to come along. We made a whole vacation out of it. We were staying in a hotel that had an indoor courtyard surrounded by rooms. In the middle of the hotel, right outside our room, there was a playground and an indoor swimming pool. The pool was walled off so it could be closed at night, but it was still open above.

It was a lot of fun for us kids. We would wake up each morning and spend as much time as we could at the playground and pool. Mom would stay in the room with the two youngest children, checking on us frequently. My dad was gone during the day for work. It was heavenly.

I think I was eleven or so. Josh, John, and I were at the pool. Mom was back in the room with Michael and Alina and had left me in charge of my brothers. We were swimming and having a great time jumping and splashing around. There were a couple of other adults there with their children, but it wasn't crowded. After a while, I got distracted and wasn't watching the boys as closely as I should have been.

I was a good swimmer, spending lots of time swimming under water. At one point, I realized I hadn't checked on them for a while. I stopped where I was and craned my neck, trying to catch sight of them across the water. I scanned the pool from end to end twice, then climbed up a few steps and surveyed the lounge chairs and tables scattered around the edge.

"Josh! John!" I called. My voice was swallowed up by the water and open air above me. I called for them again, then climbed out of the pool. They had probably just gone back to the room. I was annoyed at having to go look for them. I'd much rather swim, but I didn't want to get in trouble for not being a good babysitter.

The wall that surrounded the pool jutted inward at one point. It formed a little alcove that provided some shelter from the splashing nearer the pool. I followed this wall around, continuing to call my brothers' names. "Josh, John, where are you? Come on, you're going to be in trouble."

I heard a low sound and hurried around the corner. There they were, their backs to me. My first reaction was relief that I wasn't going to get into trouble, but then I saw a little girl, probably under five years old, backed into the corner. Her one-piece swimsuit was pulled down to her waist, and my brothers were trying to yank it down farther. She was just a tiny little thing, probably had no idea that these boys were doing something wrong. The boys didn't see me, and they had been so intent on what they were doing, they hadn't heard my voice. They laughed quietly and nudged each other.

I was frozen for a moment, my heart in my throat. Child or not, I knew they were way out of line. At first, I doubted whether I was even seeing this. How should an eleven-year-old handle a situation like that? There were no adults in direct line of sight, no one that I could signal for help. The boys didn't know I was there. I couldn't decide what to do. I wanted to rush over and stop them, but would I even be able to? Experience had shown that they were stronger than me and unflinching when they'd determined to do something.

Memories are funny things. Some of them are so crystal clear, that flashbulb picture that is burned into your mind. Yet, the details get fuzzy the further out you move from that moment. I don't remember exactly what happened after that. I think I ran for the girl's mother and then for my mother. Maybe the boys got in trouble. I'm sure there was some sort of consequence, but I don't remember much more than that.

Still, that moment stayed with me—the huddled, half-naked little girl, my laughing brothers, the sick taste in my mouth. It was the first time I saw so clearly that my brothers and I were different. What was okay to them was abhorrent to me. I found out later that they tried the same thing with Alina when she was little. It wasn't like they were five or six themselves; they were teenagers by that time. Plenty old enough to know better, to know exactly what they were doing. They weren't just rambunctious boys; they needed help. They never got it.

Josh Powell - 1991

In fact, the downward spiral only continued. According to my Aunt Becky, Josh and John physically and sexually abused Alina. Again, I never knew about that then. It wasn't until I got a copy of the divorce papers and started going through them that I first learned about it.

My Aunt Becky also related one more story that still leaves me feeling baffled and angry. Sometimes during 1989 when she was visiting my parents, she witnessed a scene that disturbed her greatly.

"It was very late at night (around midnight), and Terri came downstairs to my room very, very upset and crying that she was afraid of Joshua, and that he might stab her, as he was threatening her and was very emotionally unstable at the time. Of course I was terrified, and I also had my two-year-old baby with me. We considered calling the police or some kind of mental health place, but in the end she wanted to call my brother, Kevin, who came over and calmed her down. Her reaction to this incident indicated to me how very out of control things were and how bad they were getting there."

My mom also wrote that Josh *"became unwilling to interact, even to make eye contact for a year or two,"* and, later, that *"he tried to commit suicide."*

That Mom knew all of this and didn't fight harder infuriates me. I know I really don't understand what it was like for her being married to my dad, but I still have a hard time dealing with the fact that she stayed in that situation for so long, that she knew the trouble that her kids were having, and that she didn't push harder for a real, long-term solution. This is just one of the continuing challenges I have in dealing with the way Mom handled (or didn't handle) each situation that arose.

But the real root of these problems was with my dad.

Aunt Becky's statement declares:

> *"These boys, I fear, are going to be getting into trouble with the law sooner or later, as they have a very distorted image of their own unquestionable right to do anything they darn well please combined with a very deep contempt towards women in general and any authority at all."*

I can't imagine where they would acquire respect for women. It certainly wasn't taught in our home. My dad did everything in his power to reinforce the idea that women were nothing more than tools to fill any pleasure or desire that a man should wish.

Besides the journal detailing his obsession over the other woman, he deliberately encouraged his boys to ignore direct requests from Mom, telling them they didn't have to do anything she asked. He talked about women in disgusting ways, even sitting around the dinner table.

One day as we were having dinner with my aunt and uncle, he turned to Josh and John, who had recently returned from an overnight youth church activity.

"So, did you find any girls you lusted after?" he asked, as blasé as if talking about the weather. Mom and I were mortified. My aunt and uncle shifted in their seats, uncomfortable with the new topic. The boys had the good grace to act embarrassed, too.

"No, Dad," John said.

Dad lightly punched John on the arm. "Why not? They are all lusting after your body, after all."

If he was willing to talk like that in front of guests, you can imagine what kind of conversations went on when it was just the boys together.

Once, John used some of his money to purchase a poster of a mostly-nude model. She wore the tiniest scrap of a bikini and was posed in a sexual way. He hung it on his bedroom wall. Mom was dismayed. She insisted that he take the poster down and get rid of it. John argued, and the discussion grew quite heated. My dad stepped in to interrupt.

"You need to leave until you calm down," he said to Mom. He took her on a drive to get her out of the house. Mom appealed to him to support her in setting boundaries regarding the poster.

"No," he said. "I think you are completely out of line. John has the right to have whatever he wants hanging in his room. He purchased that poster with his own money, so it's his personal property. You can't deny him that."

"It's not ok. A picture like that sets him up to think about women like objects. I don't want it in the house."

"Well, I'm not going to take it down, and I'm not going to make John do it either. If you want it down, you are going to have to do it yourself."

The poster stayed up for years.

I read that story written in my dad's own words in the divorce papers. It was sickening to read a couple of other statements he made about Josh and John:

> *"The petitioner's parents, John and Carol Martin, interpret Josh and John's singular dedication to the development of their native talents and abilities as sociopathy."*

And later:

> *"John Martin has suggested to Josh and John that they will turn into psychopaths . . ."*

It was clear to everyone but my dad that he was setting my brothers up for a lifetime of mental illness and worse. But no one knew just how much worse it would really be.

CHAPTER FOURTEEN

Over the last few years, I've been interviewed dozens of times. Many people have asked how I turned out so different from my siblings. Each one of them, including Michael and Alina—once my sweet, little friends—have taken my dad's side and fallen prey to his lies and manipulations. Somehow, he hasn't been able to affect me the same way, something for which I am constantly grateful.

I can date my sense of clarity where my dad is concerned back to a day when I was fourteen years old. Mom was bowed under the weight of my dad's ranting, and I think she was again contemplating divorce. It had been a particularly trying day, with my dad going on and on about how everything bad in the world could be traced back to two sources: the LDS Church and the Government. He was short tempered with us kids and with Mom, insulting and commanding her in an alternating pattern that left us all drained.

At last, it was bedtime. I escaped to my room, grateful to be free from him and my brothers for a brief spell. Mom followed behind.

"Jenny, I want to talk to you," she said. She came into my room, and we sat on my bed. A feeling of companionship hung around us. Mom started talking to me about the day, our family, school—

general chatting. I don't remember all the details of the conversation, but there was one thing that stood out to me.

"Do you see the way your dad acts and speaks?" she asked. I nodded. How could I miss it? "I want you to look at his choices and try to imagine where they will lead him. Look down the road five years, ten years. Where will he end up?"

She took a deep breath and covered her face with a weary hand. We sat in silence for a moment, and when she looked up again, there was a surprising sense of peace there. Her eyes softened as she spoke the next words. "Now look at the path that Jesus Christ has laid out. What kinds of things has he asked you to do? Imagine where those choices will lead."

They were simple words, but they were almost magical. A vision of the future opened before me, stretching out into the distance as far as I could see. It was as if I were standing on a path with a fork in the road ahead. To one side stood my dad, waving me toward him. I was tempted to step closer to him. Maybe then he would finally smile at me in approval. But the path he was on became more murky and dark the further it stretched. Potholes and piles of trash littered its surface, and it sloped steadily downward. On the other side was Jesus. He opened his arms to me, full of love and an invitation to follow Him. His path was beautiful. It was bordered by flowers and forests, though it had hills and valleys of difficulty. Above all, I could feel the joy that awaited me if I chose to take it.

In that quiet, simple conversation with my mother, I realized that I had a choice. I didn't have to follow my dad's path of hate. I could accept that he would never love me, and I could choose higher ground. I knew, too, that it wasn't always easy to take that better road. The way my dad treated Mom was a prime example of the kind of opposition I would face by choosing to follow Jesus's path. But would it be worth it?

I was only fourteen years old, but I made the decision that day that would determine the course of my life. I looked down those two paths, and I chose to turn away from my dad. I decided that I was not going to follow along in his wake but would walk the other way. From that day on, it was like a curtain had been removed from my eyes. A new light had dawned, illuminating all the dark nooks and crannies that had been kept secret and hidden from view. It burst through my life and changed the way I saw my dad, the way I saw *everything*.

My dad seemed to sense my new enlightenment, and we were often at odds, as I wouldn't agree with his opinions. Our relationship declined quickly, but I never regretted my decision to separate myself from him.

Looking back, I can see that conversation as a turning point in my life. Before that day, I was powerless against my father, sometimes in his spell. After that, I had set myself firmly against the ugliness that he stood for. There was part of me that still wanted my dad to love me, to be proud of me. But I wouldn't let him change me.

It was definitely for the best that I found my new focus then. Things went rapidly downhill from there, and by the time I turned eighteen, Mom finally accepted that the marriage could not—*should* not—be saved.

She mentioned divorce occasionally, but she still didn't know how to support herself or her children, and she remained terrified of losing us. Dad knew this and played it to his advantage. He threatened her that she wouldn't get to see her boys if she left him—he wasn't interested in us girls. Meanwhile, he continued to become more and more abusive, cutting her down constantly and picking at everything she did. She was never pretty enough, frugal enough, intelligent enough for him. He mocked her in front of us and did his best to undermine her authority, especially with the boys.

It worked. The boys had no respect for her at all. When she asked them to do their schoolwork or household chores, they would blatantly refuse. My dad backed them up.

"If you don't do any cleaning, how can you expect the kids to do it? You'll just have to do it yourself," he told her. It didn't matter that she cleaned constantly. She couldn't keep up with the mess that seven people made on her own.

I remember one of the times she tried to get John to help. "John, come in here and get the dishes done," she called.

"Why should I?" he shot back from his seat on the sofa. His eyes never left the television. My dad sat next to him. He looked over at John and grinned. Mom did the dishes herself.

It was always like that, and the fighting only got worse. Anything my mom did, especially anything involving church, was considered by my dad to be cult-like. All the while, we were forced to listen to his constant harping on our most sacred beliefs.

Contrary to Mom's hopes, the divorce only escalated things for a long time. Now, each little inch was a battleground to be fought in the courts. What should have taken a few months took more than two years to complete. Court orders were needed to get my dad to move out, to get him to stop dropping by at any time of the day or night. He dug in his heels and resisted with all his might.

For quite a while, the war was over custody. Mom couldn't handle Josh and John with my dad still holding so much influence over them. They had no desire to be with her, and she accepted defeat there. They lived with my dad most of the time, coming by for visits any time they wanted. Dad had made it clear that Alina and I were second-class citizens and should stay with Mom. He said as much in front of Alina, who was only seven at the time.

"If Mom and I get a divorce," he told the boys one day, his voice casual, "I'll go rent one of those apartments down the street, and you boys will come live with me."

"What about the girls?" Michael asked. Alina was sitting nearby, and she looked up eagerly to hear her fate.

"Mom will keep the girls." He said it without any emotion. I couldn't wait to be away from him, but I can only imagine what that did to the heart of my little sister.

Michael was another story. He was one of the boys—the superior members of the family. Dad wanted him, and so did Josh and John. Michael was ten at the beginning of the divorce, and he was struggling. One minute, he would be cuddling with Mom, needing her reassurance and comfort, and the next, he'd be spouting off my dad's garbage.

"If Mom cared, she would get off her lard-butt and go out and get a job and CONTRIBUTE something." My dad's words coming out of Michael's mouth were even more disturbing than hearing them from their original source.

We noticed that when he spent a few days with us, he would gradually soften and become a happier boy, playing and laughing and acting like a normal kid should. Just a few minutes with my dad around, though, and that was all reversed.

The battle for Michael was taken to the courts. Pages and pages of statements were collected from friends and family in support of Mom as she tried everything she could to get custody of Michael. Temporary custody was awarded to her during the proceedings, and it gave her hope that she would be able to have him. Josh and John were so far under my dad's control, violent and disrespectful, that it was impossible to be around them.

But there was still hope for Michael.

One day, I was sick, so I stayed home from work. My dad still had access to the house because his office was there. He was allowed to be there during business hours, and then he was supposed to be out. Mom spent a lot of time with her family during those hours, trying to avoid my dad.

I heard my dad talking with Josh. "Maybe you should live with Mom. I don't want to leave Michael alone with Mom. She says she loves you boys, but she can't control you, so she doesn't want you."

Josh laughed. "She can't control us, but she thinks she can control Michael? How the hell does she think she can control Michael? *We* control Michael!" They both laughed then.

Another time, Michael and the boys went somewhere with my dad. When they got home, Michael was in a blistering mood. He went upstairs to see Mom. A little while later, he came stomping back down. He saw me sitting in the living room.

"Do you really like Mom?" he asked, his face all scrunched up with anger.

I sighed. "What did she do this time?"

He crossed his arms and glared. "She's *sitting* up there!"

"Oh, is that right? On what chair?" I asked with a laugh, trying to tease him out of his foul mood.

He was disgusted with my comment. "She won't get off my back."

When I asked Mom and Grandma about it, Grandma shook her head. "All she did was offer him dinner."

When the court at long last decided custody, they gave Michael to my dad. I don't know the details about that decision, what made them think that was the best solution. Maybe it was in the hopes that the fight would end and civilized behavior would resume. Or maybe my dad managed to convince them that he really was the best for Michael. I can only guess, but I have a hard time accepting that decision, even now.

Alina's was the saddest story of all, though.

John regularly referred to Alina by a foul name. She was seven years old, but she was called a b____ often by her older brother, something he'd heard his dad call his mother. He was always pushing her around, and the other boys weren't much better.

With that sort of treatment, as well as the comments my dad had made about not wanting her, it wasn't a surprise when Mom found her sitting in her room crying one day. She later wrote down the encounter.

"What's wrong, honey," Mom asked, sitting down beside her.

"Mama, I know that Daddy and the boys really don't hate me. They just act like they hate me. I know that in their hearts they really love me. Someday they'll act like they love me." Only seven years old, this little girl was desperate to have her father want her. Any time she got to go visit him or he took her somewhere, she was ecstatic, even though it meant being with her brothers, who treated her so poorly.

Now the battle was for Alina. This battle wasn't waged in the courts, but in Alina's heart. My dad fought for her allegiance. I don't know his motivation. He'd never been interested in having her before. Maybe having all three boys wasn't a good enough defeat over my mother. I guess that he knew I was forever out of his reach. That had started when I was fourteen. He saw me as "on her side," and that infuriated him. He wouldn't rest until all the other children were his.

There was no doubt that Alina would not be safe in that environment. The incident with the gerbils, the fact that Josh and John had sexually abused her in some way when she was just a tiny girl, John's constant swearing and pushing around—all of these things added up to make my dad the last person who should be in charge of her care. My mom wrote down another incident that makes me sick to my stomach. I have an eight-year-old daughter, and the thought of her, or any of my children, in an environment like this is impossible to consider.

"Just a few nights ago, Steve, Josh, and John were all gathered, harassing me. At one point, one of the boys said, 'What will we do with Alina when she comes to our house to visit and we have girls over? Oh, we'll just let her watch.' I asked, 'Watch what?' Johnny made an obvious sexual gesture and said, 'Watch us dance.' Josh said, 'Yeah, under the sheets.' They went on like this for a few minutes, then Steve finally said, 'Okay, okay, boys.'"

According to my Aunt Becky:

"[Terri] has spoken to me in regard to her fear that one of them [Josh or John] will actually kill her and/or Alina."

The divorce took two-and-a-half years. By the time it was finalized, I was married, so I don't know all the ins and outs of how things went with Alina. All I know is that eventually, she insisted that she was going to live with my dad, and that was that. I guess Mom was defeated.

She let Alina go.

Through the entire process, I felt highly protective and incredibly anxious for Mom's well-being. I would stay home from work if my dad was going to be coming over, not willing to let Mom face him alone. Beyond being a daughter of a divorcing couple, I functioned more like a best friend, trying to be there to support Mom through the experience.

Once, my dad was at the house. He started to go down the hall, saying he needed some mortgage papers. Mom wasn't about to let him just go through things on his own, so she followed him. A few minutes later, I heard her scream.

"Jenny! Help me!"

I ran into my room, followed by the boys, where Mom had some papers for the custody hearing laid out on my bed. When I got there, she was holding the papers, and my dad was grappling with her, trying to rip them from her hands. The boys jumped into the fray, trying to help my dad get the papers from her. Mom screamed and tucked them closer to her body.

"Call the police. Call 911!"

I ran to the phone and dialed. Dad and the boys backed off. They continued to try to grab the files but didn't touch her anymore.

"You don't need to call the police, Jenny," my dad said, his voice calm.

But I called anyway.

That was only one instance. Mom didn't intentionally put me in the middle, and she didn't tell me everything—a lot of these details I learned years later in going through the divorce papers. But I certainly knew enough, and I had witnessed most of it.

As a teenager, I don't remember wondering why she hadn't left him years before. She always had a reason to stay. Marriage and family were everything to her, and she didn't want to give up until there was no hope. She had said before that she had never felt the time was right. It all made sense to me then.

Now, looking back, sometimes I wonder if that feeling was a true instinct or if it was more about fear—fear about trying to support her family, fear about my dad taking the kids away from her, fear of the unknown in general. Why didn't she leave years before? Would that have changed us? Changed who Josh grew up to be?

My dad's nature was so caustic, so dividing all the time. Once the divorce began, that was just intensified. Couples going through something like that are often caught up in the most negative emotional experience of their lives, but even the lawyers commented on how nasty my dad was. He twisted everything to such an extreme that no one could recognize the original facts anymore.

At the time, I thought Mom was so strong. Now, sometimes I question if it really was strength, really patience, or if that was just fear.

I got a grant for college but decided not to go because I needed to stay and help protect Mom. That was my decision. But when I got engaged, she asked me not to get married. She still needed me.

I had to make another decision then, another turning point. My entire twisted family life could not continue to determine my future. It was time for me to step out on my own.

CHAPTER FIFTEEN

Witnessing my parents' broken marriage affected me deeply. I was determined that my future would follow a different path. When I met Kirk Graves, I was instantly impressed.

Kirk was newly returned from a mission to London, England, for the LDS Church. He had just spent two years sharing the gospel message full time, all his thoughts and efforts were focused in this one direction without the distraction of girls or making a living. It was an environment perfect for learning about service and hard work.

His family had been living in Utah when he left on his mission two years earlier, and they moved to our ward in Washington while he was gone, so I'd never met him. I'd talked to his sister about him, and everyone in the ward had heard how eagerly he was anticipated by his family.

The return of a missionary is always something to celebrate. A young man's loved ones get excited during the last few months, and Kirk's family was no exception. As a nineteen-year-old girl, I was interested to see what this much-talked-about young man would be like.

It wasn't long after he had gotten back that he captured my full attention. Kirk was intelligent, spiritual, and appeared to be a lot of fun, from the little I saw during church. And it didn't hurt that he was cute, too.

Kirk told me later that he first noticed me during the Christmas Pageant. I was playing Mary, and he couldn't take his eyes off me. He didn't ask me out right away, though. There were some major decisions to be made about where to go to complete his education, and it was a strong possibility that he would be moving back to Utah. He didn't want to start a relationship if he would only end up leaving. Now, I can see his point, but then, I'd wondered what it would take to get him to actually ask me out.

His sister Amie and I were friendly acquaintances, mostly at church. But I found an excuse to stop by and pick up a book at her house in the hopes that Kirk would be around. What should have been a five minute visit turned into ten, then fifteen minutes as I stretched the conversation out as long as possible. Finally, my ploy paid off, and Kirk came upstairs. He joined the conversation, and we continued talking for a while longer.

"Amie, I hear there is a young adult activity coming up. Would you like to go?" I glanced at Kirk. "Or we could all go?"

"That sounds like fun," Kirk replied. Amie agreed, too, and we went to the Wednesday evening activities for a couple of weeks, all three of us. One week, shortly before Christmas, Amie couldn't go, so Kirk and I went alone. It wasn't an official "date," but it was a step in the right direction.

It seemed that if something was going to happen, I would have to be the one to do it. My aunt talked me into calling him, and I got up the courage to ask him on our first date. We hit it off immediately, and it didn't take long for me to know that he was the one. For Kirk, the idea of going back to school in Utah became less and less of an option. We only dated for five weeks before we got engaged.

It was fast, but I knew it was right. Besides the fact that I was simply in love with him, Kirk was the complete opposite of my dad. He was respectful of me, fun loving, and committed to our church. He treated me well and showed deference and respect to my mom.

The only dark spot on this happy time was the fear that clawed its way to the surface at odd moments. By this time, my parents were embroiled in the heated divorce. I couldn't help but look at them and worry. Would I end up in the same position? Would I have to go through the heartache my mom was experiencing? I had built up a lot of paranoia over the years, and it wasn't always easy to trust Kirk. But Kirk was such a different man than my dad.

So we talked about it. I didn't hold back anything. I told him all about my dad and his controlling, demeaning behaviors. I talked about my absolute disgust over all forms of pornography and how important it was to me that we always stay active and involved in our church. Kirk shared his concerns about the way my parents' marriage had ended, and we made a decision that we would never, no matter what, *ever* consider getting divorced. If we were going to get married, it was going to be forever, and that meant that we would decide now to work through whatever challenges or problems came our way.

Jennifer and Kirk - 1994

We were married on August 5, 1994, in the Portland, Oregon, LDS Temple. It was the most amazing day of my life. We didn't invite my dad—who needed the drama? So everything was peaceful at the wedding. I'll never forget how it felt to know that this wonderful man was mine for eternity.

Then my dad showed up at the reception. He was fairly civil to me, but he got loud and raucous enough that my uncle had to ask him to calm down. We got through it.

We celebrated with a reception in Spokane and another in Provo, Utah, then settled in to married life.

The first few years of our marriage were difficult. The common issues that new couples face of trying to blend two backgrounds into one marriage were often exacerbated by my control issues.

There were times when we were gritting our teeth and hanging on by our fingernails, but we had made the decision to work through it, so that's what we did. Our marriage was strengthened, and we learned to love each other even more deeply.

Shortly before we were married, Mom, Kirk, and I traveled to Seattle together. Mom had finished up her massage therapy classes and needed to take the certification test. I decided that it was a good idea to use the opportunity for Kirk to meet my dad.

Kirk had heard Mom and me discuss my dad many times. I had been completely open with him about my dad's issues, but Kirk was always the kind of guy to give someone the benefit of the doubt.

He told me later that he thought, "They're just traumatized; it's been a rough road for them. He can't really be that bad." I didn't know this at the time. I had given him fair warning about what we were in for.

After the test, we drove to my dad's house, and before we had even gotten out of the car, he came toward us across the lawn and stood outside the window while he yelled at Mom. Kirk was shocked. Neither of us remembers the subject matter; it was some petty, insignificant thing. What stood out was the sheer malice that was unleashed for no apparent reason. It was an impression that stuck with Kirk forcefully. It's funny, but I hardly remember the incident. I'm sure it was so commonplace to me that it didn't make an impression other than the fact that I was embarrassed that he was acting that way in front of my fiancé.

It was a great relief for me to move to Utah, away from my dad and all of his ugliness. We started a family, and I tried to ignore my dad as much as possible. Life was good.

116

CHAPTER SIXTEEN

While I was so happily involved with my new family, Josh was going through a transition of his own. All three of my brothers had been living with my dad, and Josh seemed to be really unhappy.

Mom kept in contact with him and filled me in when we chatted every week or two. In 1998, Josh was sleeping around, living it up . . . and totally miserable. He had bought my dad's philosophy hook, line, and sinker, but was finding that it didn't bring the satisfaction that he'd always been told it would. He complained to Mom and opened up to her, more sincere than he'd been in years. After several long discussions, Mom talked him into moving back in with her for a while.

My old protective instincts kicked in. Would Josh be cruel to her again? But over the next year, Josh started what seemed to be a miraculous transformation. I could only listen in amazement as Mom described him going back to church, starting college, and in all other ways making positive changes in his life. Getting away from my dad was working for him. I began to have hope that he would see the link between action and consequence like I had all those years before.

He stayed with my mom for a year and then got an apartment with a couple of roommates and moved back to Puyallup. He continued that forward momentum. He was pursuing a business degree at Washington State and attending the local LDS singles' ward.

And that is where he met Susan.

Susan was eighteen, just out of high school, and Josh was six years older. He was going to Washington State with a major in Business, and he worked for the same furniture company as my dad. He seemed confident and involved and had a plan for the future. She was smitten with him.

A few years later, Susan and I were chatting about her early relationship with Josh.

"He was always so romantic." She sighed.

I laughed. "Really? That's hard to picture."

"No, it's true. He really was. He used to bring me flowers and kiss me so passionately. I felt truly loved back then."

But however Susan felt, Chuck and Judy were concerned. They didn't know Josh well, but the few interactions they'd had showed him to be completely selfish and full of himself. Susan often stayed out late, and her parents were disturbed by the fact that Josh didn't have any problem sending his girlfriend home alone at one or two in the morning. They thought that it looked bad and wondered that he didn't act bothered about her safety.

Josh and Susan's Engagement Photo- 2001

To those who had known Josh for years, this behavior seemed like a vast improvement in character, but for Chuck and Judy, who were looking out for the safety and happiness of their daughters, a man like Josh was bad news.

In January of 2001, Josh and Susan asked her family over for dinner at his apartment. It was clear that they had some big news but wanted it to be a surprise. After dinner, Josh asked everyone to come sit down in the living room. He set up his video camera and then got down on one knee and proposed to Susan. Chuck later said it was as if he was proposing to the camera since it was obviously not a surprise to Susan.

Chuck described their wedding in April as follows:

Josh and Susan's Wedding
April 6, 2001

"Josh and Susan's wedding was a complete mess, to the extent that Josh was involved in the planning or execution of the wedding, but we did our best to ignore the problems. Josh and "his family" met us in Portland at the temple; April 6, 2001. Susan went inside while Josh, his father, and his youngest sister Alina took pictures outside the temple. Josh kept saying, "Just one more photo, just one more." I had to take his arm and his camera and walk him into the temple for the ceremony. Susan was inside and waiting. Josh's dad tried to go inside even though he knew he would not be allowed to go in, due to his lack of worthiness. They left for a honeymoon after the wedding and were to be back in Puyallup for the reception the next day. They were three hours late, but it didn't seem to bother Josh. My daughter Susan overheard Josh's dad saying, "She isn't a doctor or lawyer, but she'll do." They had been seriously talking about marrying a woman who could financially support her husband. Susan was offended, but pretended she hadn't heard it. She did confide this to her mother at a later date. Josh also argued with the

professional wedding photographer, and in the end, we have almost no pictures; Josh has them all."

Josh and I had reconnected some by this time because he had changed so much. He called occasionally. He called about meeting Susan and asking her to marry him. It seemed like he wanted the kind of life that I had. So they chose the Portland Temple because that's where I'd been married, and they honeymooned their first night together at the same hotel on the water; the beautiful location that Kirk and I'd gone to.

Whatever anyone else's feelings, Susan was excited to start their life together. Josh went back to work, and Susan started at beauty school. Money was tight, and Josh talked to Chuck about it, hoping for a loan. Chuck wanted him to learn to support his family and suggested that maybe he could take on a few more assignments at work. Josh didn't like that idea. Shortly after that, he quit his job, protesting that the company was going to reduce the amount they paid their installers for their mileage. That left him unemployed. I guess it was better, in his mind, to have no income than to work harder and take on more installation jobs.

One of Josh's more difficult traits was his desire to wring every last drop of perceived value from a purchase. This showed up clearly in a dispute he had with the apartment complex they were living in. There had been an annoying noise in a vent that Susan and Josh both thought was a trapped bird. Josh went to the managers and told them that they needed to install some kind of outside vent cover. The management didn't do it. This was a big enough deal to him, apparently, that he decided to stop paying rent and gathered a group of other tenants to sue the owners of the property.

On an even stranger note, Josh decided to act as the attorney, not only for himself, but for the entire group. He read through the state laws and figured that he knew enough to represent their case well. It was always very important to him to be taken seriously in whatever new plan he had concocted. He even started talking about taking the bar exam, feeling that he wouldn't even need law school in order to pass. He knew enough already.

He lost the case and was ordered to pay a $1200 judgment. They were forced to move out of the apartment.

Josh went through a number of different jobs. He got hired on fairly easily, but then, within a few weeks, he would quit or get fired. It was always the same story. The people he was working for didn't know what they were doing. He was so much more qualified than they were, and he couldn't stand to work for people whose standards weren't as high as his. In the end, he always ended up staying at home and managing the money that Susan brought in.

Eventually, Josh finished his bachelor's degree in business. At least, that's what he told people. Many years later, after all the news coverage, research was done, and no record of Josh's degree could be found. His family and friends had no reason to doubt him then, however.

With his "degree" under his belt, Josh got a job managing retirement facilities, and Susan also got a job working there. He was in charge of giving tours of the different facilities, signing up new residents, and managing the staff. It was a great option for them. They lived in an apartment for free on one of the properties, and all their utilities were paid for. They put their entire paychecks into savings for a while and seemed to be doing well. Susan enjoyed the work and was well liked by the residents, but Josh started again to question the decisions of his employers. Eventually, he pushed it too far and was fired. Since the job required a husband and wife team, they were both out of work and out of a place to live.

It was at this time that they moved in with my dad. There were already three other grown children living with him, and space was limited, but they didn't really have any other options. They moved into the dining room, hanging sheets around for some extra privacy. Josh seemed perfectly content with the arrangement, but Susan was miserable.

My dad had often made Susan feel uncomfortable, and she later expressed to me that she felt like he was spying on her. Josh was oblivious, and Susan wondered if maybe she was just being paranoid, but then my dad approached her with a very disturbing offer.

One day, she was sitting in the car with him, waiting for Josh to come out of the house, when he turned to her. I don't know the exact words he used, but the essence was that he was in love with her, and he knew she felt the same. He was sure that he and Josh could share her as their common wife.

She told me about the interchange in a telephone conversation. "I told him, 'No way.' I couldn't even believe he would say something like that," she said on the phone. She acted a little hesitant to share the story. After all, we didn't yet know each other well.

My stomach twisted painfully. "Wow, he's gotten much worse. He's been messed up for a long time, but I wouldn't have expected him to let it go as far as his own daughter-in-law." I explained briefly about his obsession with that other woman from years ago. "I'm so sorry you're dealing with this."

"Thanks," she said. We sat in silence for a minute. We'd only met at the wedding and a couple of times since then, and we were hardly close. But now we were talking about things of a deep and disturbing nature. I felt a sudden swell of compassion for her, caught in this situation.

"Susan, you need to get away from him. My dad is twisted. I'd get out of there fast if I were you." A thought occurred to me. "You know, you could come and stay with us; move to Utah and start fresh."

She didn't answer at first, but then she drew a long breath. "I'd need to talk to Josh."

She had told Josh what had happened, and Josh had been outraged . . . at first. He confronted his father and told him to leave Susan alone. But it was all too soon that our dad had Josh convinced that Susan had made the whole thing up.

"She has too much influence over you. She's trying to control you and drive a wedge between us," he said.

In fact, the opposite was true. There was a constant tug-of-war going on between Susan and my dad. It was obvious that the more time Josh spent with him, the worse he got. I can only imagine the kind of conflicts that she had to deal with. I heard a little about it, but mostly we talked about her and Josh coming to live with us. The discussions went on for a few more weeks.

It was hard for Susan to think about moving away from her parents. But they lived only five minutes away from my dad, and she could see there would be no way to enforce limits to exposure with my dad without putting some real distance between them.

Finally, she called. It was official: Josh and Susan were moving to Utah. I was flooded with relief—and a healthy dose of apprehension, too. I had seen second hand how that year away from my dad had improved Josh so dramatically, and I hoped that this move would do the same. But I wasn't blind to the fact that we were going to be bringing all of his issues into our home.

Still, I was excited about the idea of Susan coming here. We were starting to develop a friendship. I had hopes that we would become great friends, and that Josh and Susan would be strengthened in their own marriage as well.

In December 2003, we shuffled bedrooms, moving the kids around to make room. Josh and Susan arrived, and we settled them into the room across the hall from Kirk and me.

It was a transition, of course, but it was for the best. I kept telling myself that as I saw more and more of the way Josh treated Susan.

I wrote in my journal shortly after they moved in about his attitude toward her.

> *"They came here in trouble. Marriage trouble, but I think they'll be all right. I've been giving Susan ideas, and she's very willing to hear and do. Josh, on the other hand, will have to learn by example. He treats her very poorly. He wants his way always. He lives in his own little world with his own schedule, and Susan had better just comply. Watching them interact last week, I would have said if I was a stranger looking on that Josh didn't even like her by the way he spoke to her."*

It's surprising reading that journal entry because I didn't remember it was that bad, that early. Reading it brought back lots of memories from that time.

I remember sitting in the car with Susan and another good friend, talking about Josh. Susan was saying that things were hard, and she didn't know what to do about it.

It went beyond normal marital problems that every couple has. Josh was controlling and didn't bother to try to be nice or polite about it. He spoke to Susan like she was the antagonist. Often, she was snippy or short in return, but Josh was always far worse.

Living with him was difficult. Kirk didn't like Josh and did his best to avoid him. It was hard to listen to Josh building himself as the expert on every subject, and it was intolerable the way he talked to his wife. I often felt caught in between the two men. It wasn't like Kirk was trying to put me in a difficult situation. He just didn't have the vested interest in helping Josh to put up with his crap. Josh was my brother, not his. After the first few weeks of trying to be a good example and being as patient as possible, Kirk retreated, staying in our room most of the time when Josh was around.

It was difficult all the time, but when Josh talked to our dad, it always got worse.

On March 6, 2004, I wrote in my journal:

"Josh talked to Dad two nights ago, and we've felt it ever since. He turned so mean." Then I asked myself this question: "How can I keep from becoming enemies with my brother when he treats others so poorly? Sometimes I really want to slap him!"

That week, they had finalized the purchase of their new house—a little rambler in West Valley City. They had originally planned to move out the next day, and I was lost in daydreaming about rearranging my house, deep cleaning, and getting some normalcy back in our routines. Susan and I had become close friends during the few months they'd been with us, and we would continue that friendship, but she was as eager as I was for her own space.

It took two more weeks, however, for them to finish painting, and then they moved in. Susan was so excited to at last have her own home after so much bouncing around. She was optimistic about settling down. Surely, this would have a positive effect on their marriage.

CHAPTER SEVENTEEN

Contrary to Susan's hopes, nothing improved with the move. Josh was unstable when it came to work. He tried his hand at different things. He didn't get along well with other people, which made it hard for him to continue in employment with any one company for long. And anything he tried, he immediately became the world's foremost expert. He built a couple of websites and talked about doing that full time, but then he would fizzle out.

His next venture was real estate. He sold a couple of houses and did okay for a while, but then he decided that he was the ultimate expert. He took out a full-page color ad in the Yellow Pages, to the tune of $80,000. Instead of focusing on the sound principles of business, his focus was on making his website look cool, buying thank-you gifts for clients, designing clever sales pitches. Almost none of his time was spent in trying to actually sell houses and work with the clients he already had.

His idea of self-employment was to do whatever he wanted. As long as he looked busy, he seemed to think that was enough. This left the financial burden up to Susan. She had a job working at Wells Fargo and enjoyed it, but big changes were coming their way.

In the summer of 2004, Susan found out she was pregnant. Kiirsi and John Hellewell lived nearby, and Susan and Kiirsi had quickly become close friends. Susan couldn't wait to share the news with her.

Kiirsi told me about Josh's strange reaction.

"When they first moved in, Josh and Susan were all cute and cuddly together. Another friend used to tell them, 'Get a room.' But when Susan told him she was pregnant, it was like a switch had flipped. Suddenly, he wouldn't touch her. He treated her like she was disgusting, like there was an alien inhabiting her body. He accused her of faking the pregnancy: 'You're just making it up so you don't have to work.' Another time, he said, 'if there is something in there, I didn't do it.' Susan would get offended, of course. She offered to show him a pregnancy test or take him with her to the doctor, but he just refused."

As time went on, it was obvious, of course, that Susan actually was pregnant. Even though Josh was being horrid about it, Susan was on cloud nine. She read all the baby and parenting books she could get hold of and tried to stay healthy. She wanted to give her baby the best start in life possible.

She continued to be the primary source of income for the family, though. As her pregnancy advanced, that nagging money question became a little more worrisome. She talked about it with Chuck. She was going to need to take some time off, after all. How would they get by?

Chuck tried to talk Josh into taking a full-time job and doing real estate on the side, but Josh wasn't convinced. He was always sure that he was right around the corner from that *big break*. Then he would be rich. Until then, it was Susan's job to support them.

Susan stayed optimistic most of the time, though. With Charlie on the way, she had great things to look forward to. There was also the hope that having a child would help her marriage. She talked about it all the time. Once the baby was born, maybe Josh would want to put more effort into work. Once the baby was born, maybe Josh would think she was beautiful again. Once the baby was born . . .

Her parents came to visit when she got close to her due date. Chuck said:

"We stayed with Josh and Susan, sleeping on the floor in their Sarah Circle house. After staying up very late watching a season of the show "24," which Josh and Susan had borrowed from friends, Susan began going into labor. We waited until ten in the morning, when Susan's water broke, and it was time to go. Josh was not concerned; he could not be bothered, because he was working on a real estate form on his computer that he wanted to use on his web site. We really needed to get to the hospital, so Susan, her mother, and I left. Josh said he just had to back up some things on the computer, and he would be right there.

"We got to the hospital, and Susan was admitted. At about noon, Josh arrived with his laptop. Josh sat down in the hospital room near the window, about six feet from the foot of the bed, and started working on his laptop. My wife was comforting Susan, so I went over to see what Josh was working on—it was the same form. By about 9:30 p.m., Susan was nearing delivery and was in intense pain. Josh was still working on the laptop. Having been through the delivery experience with my four children, I realized that this was a critical time. I went over to Josh and told him, "You need to put down the laptop now and go help your wife; she needs you." Josh finally put down the laptop. I told him to go stand by the bed and hold Susan's hand. Susan was very relieved he had come to support her. Josh looked pale and became emotionally involved. He appeared to finally realize just how intense this was for Susan.

The baby was delivered within thirty minutes. Susan then began to praise Josh for being there when she needed him. Josh was glad to hold the new baby and was proud to show off the baby, and I felt that perhaps he might do okay as a father and husband."

And in many ways, it seemed like that hope might come true. To the casual observer looking on from the outside, Josh was a happy father. He gave the impression that he was opening up a bit more. He was more affectionate to Susan than he'd been during her pregnancy, and he held Charlie and appeared to be proud of his son.

But to those of us who were close to Susan and Josh, we could see that nothing much had really changed. Beyond holding Charlie, Josh didn't do anything to help care for his son. Susan was breastfeeding, so Josh couldn't feed him, but unless Susan insisted, he didn't change diapers or help with housework or laundry. The burden of caring for the new baby fell entirely on Susan.

She had taken time off of work after Charlie was born, but she really wanted to stay home full time and raise her son. That wasn't much of a possibility with Josh not bringing in a steady income.

Still, even after she went back to work, Susan was absolutely joyful in being a mother. She was extremely attentive to Charlie. When she welcomed Braden into their family two years later, she was radiant. She took great pains to care for all of their needs.

Susan, Charlie and Braden – July 2008

She was always trying to get Josh more involved with the boys. She encouraged him to read bedtime stories to them, and sometimes he would do it. The boys always loved to have him read to them, but he wasn't very consistent.

Daycare was a big issue for her. It was hard enough to be away from her boys every day. Since Josh was home during the day, the boys stayed home with him for a while, but Josh tended to ignore them. Coming home to find diapers that had needed to be changed for hours and no signs that they'd been fed—she couldn't keep that up. She started looking for a new child care situation right around the same time that Josh got a job.

He was hired to work as an accountant a bit farther south from my house, so it was the perfect arrangement for me to watch the boys. For four months, Charlie and Braden came to my house four days a week. They were sweet, darling little boys, and I thoroughly enjoyed them, even though it added a lot of work to caring for my own five children. They seemed really happy to be here, and Kristen adored helping me care for them.

After only a couple of months, Josh lost his job. He claimed that he had wanted to leave anyway. The owners had no idea how to run a business . . . they wouldn't listen to any of his suggestions . . . he had another opportunity with someone else who would appreciate him. It was the same story as always before. In the end, I'm pretty sure he was fired. He found another job rather quickly that was farther north from me.

At that point, my house was too much out of the way, and Susan was back to scrambling, trying to figure out what to do for child care for her boys.

This was about the time that she found Debbie Caldwell. She lived close to their home and was a sweet woman who ran a polished, professional daycare in her home. She was trained and certified, warm and affectionate. The boys took to her immediately, and so did Susan. With her parents far away, Debbie became almost like a grandmother to the boys and another mother figure to Susan.

Debbie told me later that when Susan came to meet with her the first time, they had an interesting conversation. Josh had come with her and was in the backyard with the boys. Susan had asked all her questions about rates and times, but Debbie could tell she still had something else she wanted to ask.

"So, how would you feel about working with me if I ended up being a single mom?"

Debbie wasn't sure exactly what to say. "Is that likely?"

"Well, things are rocky with my husband, and it's possible that we may get divorced."

I don't remember much more of her description, but that much stuck with me. At the very least, she and Susan became close quickly, and Charlie and Braden had a safe place to be cared for while Susan was at work.

Debbie wasn't the only one Susan took into her confidence. She had friends at work she confided in, and she talked to both Kiirsi and I. Things were not good with Josh, and they were getting worse.

Josh was in contact much more with my dad. They talked on the phone at least two or three times a week. Each phone call would last for up to four hours. When he got off the phone, he would always be horribly mean. He would start nitpicking her about making more money, being a better housekeeper, cooking better food—all of which she was supposed to do while working full time and caring for the boys single handedly. And not spending a dime. It was the same sort of attitude my dad had always displayed toward Mom. It was clear, at least to me, that my dad was feeding each and every line to Josh, deliberately driving a wedge in his marriage.

And Josh's controlling tendencies were getting worse. He had always had a leaning to OCD behaviors, but now it intensified. He didn't like touching other people, his wife and children included. Kissing and any type of physical relationship with Susan were especially hot topics. It was all about the germs. Poor Susan; she was an affectionate woman, and she was starved for his attention.

Then there were all of his strange doomsday statements:

"We're going to need to move to a state that has more water because eventually the world is going to run out of water."

Or

"We're not going to buy groceries anymore. If we can't grow it in our garden, we can't eat it."

Or

"Eventually, we're going to have to leave the country because the economy is so bad."

He blamed their problems on the Republicans, on the economy, on the environment—anything other than himself. When Susan tried to find ways to work through their issues, he shot every idea down.

They couldn't go to counseling because it would cost too much money. When Susan pointed out that their insurance would cover it, he refused anyway. "Then it'll show up on our records, and we'll get branded with pre-existing conditions."

If that wasn't enough, his control over the money was beyond strict. Susan's paycheck was deposited directly into the bank account, and Josh took charge of it from there. Susan had to clear any purchase she made with him. Including groceries, shoes and clothes for the boys, gas for the car—everything.

One of their biggest fights occurred after Susan told Josh she was going to the grocery store. He told her she could spend thirty dollars. Once there, she remembered some other things she needed, and she found some good bargains, so she ended up spending ninety dollars. According to Josh, this was an unforgivable betrayal.

She often struggled to even provide enough food to feed her boys. During the summer, it was a bit easier because of the garden she planted and cared for. But produce from the garden could only go so far in feeding two growing boys.

When Susan tried to make any changes to the bank account, Josh would change passwords, locking her out of accessing the money at all.

Once, Susan asked him, "Why is that you are allowed to spend money on anything for your business, but I don't get to buy groceries?"

"It's none of your business what I spend."

Susan brought up the fact that they maxed out her credit card to pay their IRA's; she wanted to start paying the credit card off. He said, "No, that's none of your business."

"How can my own credit not be my business?"

"It just works better if I handle all the expenses and the money; that's the way it works."

"Plenty of people have separate accounts and make it work," she said.

"No, it doesn't work."

And, as far as he was concerned, that was the end of the discussion.

And over it all, the threat hovered that if she did anything to fight back, he would take the boys away from her. It wasn't a blatant threat—it was more implied. But Susan knew enough about our parents' divorce, not to mention my dad's parents' kidnapping game, to make her truly afraid.

Susan and I still saw each other regularly, and she also sent me emails, keeping me posted on how things were going. In June of 2008, a full eighteen months before she went missing, she sent me an email that she called her "deposition." It detailed all of the issues that she and Josh were having. It was obvious that she was starting to set things in motion in the event of a divorce. She later told me she'd spoken to a couple of lawyers (free consultations only, of course) to get some advice about how she would need to proceed.

But she kept holding on. She tried to get him to go to counseling. He refused. She tried to get him to go to church; he said he'd go once a month if she would miss once a month. She agreed, but it only lasted for two months before he stopped going altogether. Yet he still expected her to skip church every fourth Sunday.

Even with all of the communication, with all of her complaints and stresses, it never occurred to me that she could be in actual physical danger. During that time was the exchange she had with Josh when she'd hit him, but even that didn't make me think he would really harm her. I hadn't read through all the divorce papers yet, so I didn't know much of his violent history. I worried more about the example that her boys were being subjected to in their father. I'd seen how my dad's influence had managed to spread like a virus to my siblings. It broke my heart to think of sweet Charlie and Braden growing up to be as messed up as their dad and grandpa were.

Susan's dad, Chuck, came for a visit during 2008. He was disturbed to realize how bad things had become. Josh had never been a favorite with Chuck; his treatment of Susan wouldn't allow for that. But now, Chuck started to get truly concerned.

He wanted her to keep in touch, but it was hard for her. When she was at work, she couldn't spend much time on the phone; at home, Josh was always around. When Chuck suggested she get a cell phone, she shook her head. Josh would never allow that. I can't imagine how Chuck must have felt to have his daughter in that situation. He wanted to make sure that she at least had a reliable way to call for help if she needed it. When he left to go back to Washington, Susan had a new cell phone provided by her parents.

This same cell phone was later found without a SIM card in Josh's car the day after Susan disappeared.

PART THREE:

THE FIGHT FOR CHARLIE AND BRADEN

"What would befall these children?
What would be their fate,
who now are looking up to me
for help and furtherance?"

-Henry Wadsworth Longfellow, *A Shadow*

CHAPTER EIGHTEEN

In the months after Susan's disappearance, we began to face the real challenge of losing a loved one. Those first terrifying moments of suspecting my brother was a killer were almost small compared to the constant day-in, day-out work of uncertainty.

And it *was* work. My heart was continually burdened by fear. There was so much to be afraid of. How much had Susan suffered? What exactly had Josh done to her? Then, a new, sickening thought occurred to me. What if she wasn't really dead? What if she was alive and being held captive somewhere? The thought of my spunky sister-in-law being abused was almost worse than thinking she was dead. My mind would race from one scenario to the other in an ever-constricting circle until I thought I would go crazy.

How did I go on from day to day? How did I get up each morning after Susan's disappearance, eat meals, and clean my house? I'm not sure I know all the answers to that question. I know that Kirk and my faith played a huge role, and Jes was there to support me through those first couple of months. But I also think it helped that only bits of the truth came to me at a time.

Even so, I was plagued by guilt. Maybe I should have seen this coming. Maybe I should have done more to encourage her to leave

Josh. Maybe I should have called her that Sunday. Maybe, maybe, maybe . . .

A burden is easier to bear when it is gradually increased. That's how it had been with my childhood, that's how it was now.

I had no idea then that Susan had written what she called her "Last Will and Testament" and placed it in a safety deposit box. At the end of that letter, Susan stated, "If Susan Powell dies, it may not be an accident, even if it looks like one." She continued on, saying that if she was dead, the police should contact me for information. I didn't learn of this until two years later. If I had known about it then, I can only imagine that the guilt could have destroyed me. At least, now I can think of that letter with gratitude. Gratitude that she trusted me enough to know I would always stand by her.

But there was little to be grateful for as January slipped into February. Then spring came, and still we had no real news about the case. The boys, so far away in Washington, were little fires that burned in the back of my mind every second of the day. The state of Utah would continue to have jurisdiction over the boys for six months after they moved to Washington. I was on tenterhooks constantly, waiting for the call that Josh had been arrested and the boys had been removed from his custody. In that case, they would be brought back to Utah. Back to our home to be cared for.

I had failed in keeping Susan safe. I could *not* fail her boys.

But though it appeared to most of us that there was plenty of evidence, that final piece of the puzzle, Susan's body, was still missing. According to my understanding, she couldn't be proven dead—therefore, Josh couldn't be charged with her murder.

So we waited.

As painful as the thought was, finding her body would be a blessing. It would give some peace of mind, knowing she was truly beyond harm, and it would answer so many questions. But even more than that, it would force the case to move ahead and hopefully get the boys away from Josh and my dad.

Every time I thought about them there, those flames in the back of my mind would roar to life, crackling with worry. I knew all too well what kind of lies and prejudices they were being exposed to. Taking away their mother would never be enough for Josh. He would try to eradicate every good thing she had tried to teach them.

The six-month mark ticked closer, and my stress level ratcheted up as every day went by without news. I kept myself together by making plans for when the boys would come live with us.

On Easter morning I took Kirk to the airport early in the morning for a business trip. It was a snowy day, but my snow tires kept me firmly attached to the pavement. I was heading back on the highway when a sedan hit a patch of ice and started to spin. It slammed into the back side of my van.

The other driver and I were both fine. But I knew as soon as she hit me that my van was totaled. When the insurance paid out for the accident, the choice before us was clear. Our family of seven already maxed out the seats in our minivan. Once Charlie and Braden came to live with us, we would need a larger car anyway. So we bought a big van, looking forward to the time when two of the empty seats would be filled.

Shortly after that, a neighbor was getting rid of a set of bunk beds. An email went around asking if anyone in the neighborhood wanted them. Here was one more thing we would need for the boys, so I contacted my neighbor, and we picked up the beds. The bedroom that had once been Josh and Susan's now was set aside for their children.

In everything we did, we tried to look forward to the future. It was so much better than looking to the past and wondering what more we could have done.

But the wait continued.

Chuck and Judy had been able to see the boys during the holidays once or twice, but then Josh had cut them off. He said they would have to email him to set up appointments to see the boys, but then he ignored their emails. They would stop by, trying to check on the boys, but no one ever answered the door.

On April 10, 2010, the first professional search took place in Utah's west desert. It was big news. Every station in both Utah and Washington carried the story, and there were lots of people interested in volunteering. The search was restricted, however, to those who had been trained. We were all very hopeful. Chuck and Judy talked about coming down to help, but then they were contacted by Josh after weeks of silence.

Josh proposed that Chuck and Judy meet them at a park for a visit with the boys. It just happened to be on the same day at the same time as the search in Utah. No matter how suspicious it seemed, Chuck and Judy jumped at the chance.

Chuck described this visit in an email to Kirk and me. Though nothing dramatic occurred during the visit, Chuck's description of Josh helped to paint a picture of the way he interacted with the boys. To one not acquainted with my brother and my father, it might help to get a glimpse into everyday life with them:

> *We were at a park with a super playground, a small lake, and plenty of people. Josh met us there by himself, and about twenty minutes later, his dad and Michael showed up. They just "happened" to be in the neighborhood and thought they might just swing by.*

The visit started out nicely, the boys playing happily on the crowded playground and bringing their grandparents little treasures—pebbles, sticks, pinecones—to hold for them. They played for an hour and a half and then started gathering up their belongings to take the boys for a snack.

> *Judy suggested we needed to go down by the lake before we left, so we started moving that way. Braden led the group with Steve Powell running behind "to keep him safe." Evidently, Steve doesn't understand that children will continue to push boundaries so long as you stay close, effectively moving the boundary. If you want them to come toward you, you have to walk away from them. Anyway, Josh had broken out the camera about one hour into "our visit," and the photo-op began. "Charlie, go stand by the goose; Braden, hug Charlie; Braden, stand over there." So we spent the next hour and a half watching the photo shoot, Josh with his camera, Steve Powell with the video camera. I had some issues with how Josh was "not" watching the boys. "Charlie, stand by the goose." Doesn't he know a goose can be mean, and they should not be chased by little boys? Doesn't he know that the closer a little boy gets to a goose, the more likely he will be to get too close, unless you're in a petting zoo? Also, the goose was over by a table of people trying to eat lunch, and you need to respect other people's space.*

Josh didn't.

Braden was wandering and found a woman and her dog. He made himself at home, playing with the woman's belongings and the dog's ball. At first, my dad tried to intervene, but Braden nagged at Josh until he gave in.

> *"Josh was totally unconcerned with Braden's boldness and imposing on another person's property, time, or space. Braden moved in, sitting on the woman and again began picking up her possessions. Josh told Braden not to take other people's things and realized he needed to get him away. Braden picked up the dog's ball (a chewed tennis ball two feet from the woman), and Josh seemed to think that was okay, and that the ball had been abandoned by someone, until the woman said, 'Oh, that's the dog's ball.' So he gave it back to the woman."*

The boys then saw some men fishing at the lake and decided they wanted to join in. Josh talked three different men into letting the boys try out their fishing rods, snapping pictures all the time. Each man was nice enough but soon retreated from the imposing family. Chuck and Judy were disgusted with the whole visit. They never got a chance to truly connect with their grandsons, and it was yet another example of the way that Josh treated people.

> *"Basically, it was the boys playing; Josh, Michael, and Steven taking pictures; while Judy and I held twigs, pinecones, and garbage/treasure the boys collected. There was no opportunity to talk with the boys, or Josh, or Steve—it was just letting us see the boys play at a public park. Josh was himself, over-imposing on everyone, thinking he was being fair and reasonable, so he felt he did well. I resisted the urge to . . . well, I resisted several urges that would not have made for a civil outing. We did take comfort in the thought that, at some point, Josh will be in jail, and we will be able to influence the boys, so live it up, Josh, Steve . . . live it up."*

Those were my sentiments, too. And this was only one little thing. Josh was always annoying. Josh and my dad being cruel and poisonous in their attitudes, that's what I was really afraid of.

Sadly, nothing came from the search in the desert. Other searches continued to take place, but as the first of July rolled around, I had to face it. The six months were up. No matter what happened now, no matter how quickly or slowly the case progressed, it was going to take a lot more legal work to get the boys away from Josh.

That six-month mark began a new state of being for me. It was the closing of a chapter in which all I had to do was wait. The police would take care of things and the boys would come to live with us. Even the preparations that I had made had been somewhat reactionary. They were small steps. Now we would have to move forward in the court system. We'd hired a lawyer a few months before, but now we talked to him again to gauge our options.

They weren't many. So much still depended on Susan's case. We couldn't force the boys away from Josh when there was no legal reason for it.

Up until this point, I had been afraid to leave the state to visit Kirk's family or take a vacation or anything. When Kirk's parents got back from a mission to Argentina, we traveled to Denver to visit them and welcome them home. I was a nervous wreck the whole time. I was so sure that as soon as we left, the police would need to bring the boys to us. What would happen to them if we weren't available? I *needed* to be there for them.

Surprisingly, the pressure lessened on me now that we were in this new chapter. Well, it didn't exactly lessen, but it changed. We were still in crises mode, but there was a sense of being able to move forward in small things. It was still hard to make long-term plans. The feeling that change was imminent started to fade. We realized that we were in this for the long haul.

At least now I would have some notice if Josh was arrested. Washington would have jurisdiction, and Chuck and Judy would become the immediate caretakers. That was a relief. The bonds we had formed with Susan's parents were all the more important now as we worked together to make sure we kept Susan's boys safe.

CHAPTER NINETEEN

For the next year, we were trapped in a never ending crisis mode. We never knew when the next event would occur. Every few weeks, there would be a hint of some new development in the case, and we would be bombarded with media calls. If there was ever a body found, they would call, wanting a response in case it turned out to be Susan. I did my best to stay connected to the television and newspaper reporters who came back to the case whenever there was a lull in other news, as well as any time the police issued any kind of statement about Susan's disappearance.

It was emotionally draining work. I was always being asked how I felt about this clue or the other. What could I say? I tried to be as open and honest as I could, but it took its toll. There was no chance to catch our breath and recover. We never felt like things were settling down.

Chuck, Judy, Kiirsi, Kirk, and I all appeared in many interviews, both local and national. We were on Good Morning America, The Today Show, Dr. Phil, Dateline, and 20/20, as well as in every newspaper and on every TV channel in Utah and Washington. Websites like weblsueths.com and support pages on Facebook and other social media platforms all took our time as well. And it was needed. We wanted Susan's name and face in the media. The more that people remembered her, the better chance that we would find answers.

And I wanted Josh to feel the pressure.

Josh and my dad had started to get more vocal in their efforts to slander Susan. They had started a website, www.susanpowell.org, during the summer. It was filled with saccharine pleas for Susan to come home to them. I had seen the site and had been disgusted by it, but it was nothing more than another testament to the twisted way my brother and father's minds worked.

But through the summer and fall months, the site grew more antagonistic.

"Mormon's Mobilize," one page was titled. It went on in a diatribe about how Susan's friends, specifically Chuck and Judy and my family, were all Mormon, and that any smidge of accusation directed toward Josh was fabricated out of our anger that he had left the Church.

"The proficiency of the Mormon Church to organize and motivate people to action can be used for positive purposes, such as when church members help people with moving or with home repairs. However, this solidarity also motivates individuals to cover for fellow Mormons and attack perceived critics of Mormonism," the site read. It seemed to be their opinion that anyone who was a member of our church was somehow hiding the truth of what really happened.

It was ludicrous, and anyone who personally knew Susan or Josh would have been able to see through it. Not to mention the massive family cover up that was going on in an effort to protect Josh.

There were pages and pages of attacks on me, on Chuck and Judy. Most of the time, I simply ignored it. I was used to that sort of behavior from my dad.

But then they started to shout a new theory about what really happened to Susan. My dad had mentioned the idea that she had run off with another man before. But now he presented his theory as fact—Susan had left Josh and her children for a man named Steven Koecher. This man had disappeared from southern Utah about a week after Susan did.

Of course, there was nothing to connect them to each other. They'd never met, didn't have any friends in common, lived six hours away from each other, and had disappeared at different times, and yet he thought he had an ironclad argument.

He started to draw all sorts of bizarre parallels, saying that it was eerie how closely they were connected.

"Steven Koecher is a singer and songwriter, according to his friends and family. Steven Koecher also plays the guitar. Susan Powell has always been interested in music and musical talents. Josh Powell's ability to play the piano is a talent that Susan found attractive. Susan Powell's father, Chuck Cox, plays the guitar," he cited on his website. He went on to include statements about how they both like the outdoors. And they were both Mormon, of course.

But my personal favorite "connection" was that Steven Koecher had lived in Brazil for two years, so he must speak Portuguese, and "Susan Powell frequently said that she inherited her beautiful olive complexion from Portuguese ancestors. Susan often said she wants to learn to speak Portuguese."

That was so laughable to me that I wanted to stand up and shout to the world, "Well, there you go. All of the mysteries are now resolved. We can all rest in peace."

I couldn't believe he thought he could actually convince people with such a tissue-thin argument.

And it made me so angry to hear him maligning Susan that way. Even if, in some freakish accident of time and place, Susan had ever been in the same vicinity as Steven Koecher, the idea that she would run away and leave her two beautiful boys was asinine—especially knowing that they would be left with Josh as their only parent.

Even with all of this going on, the weeks and months dragged by at a snail's pace. Searches continued in the west desert, but nothing was found.

At the end of July in 2011, Kirk and I went out to lunch with Detective Maxwell and Sergeant Bobrowski to talk about the case. We chatted for a bit about my mom.

"Has she contacted you with any information yet?" I asked. I knew she still talked to Josh and my other siblings from time to time, and I had been constantly encouraging her to tell the police whenever they talked. Maybe he would let something small slip that would be a clue. I figured it wasn't our job to decide what was important or not, but that we should just relay all conversations and let the police sort it out.

Maxwell shook his head. "No, not at all. She came to that one interview but has never followed up with any more information."

I found myself clenching my jaw. This was a constant source of contention between my mother and me. She was still living with us, but we were more and more distant every day that this dragged on. She was in a continual state of denial. The fact that Josh hadn't been arrested was proof to her that he was innocent. Or maybe it was simply easier to stay complacent and pretend her son was a victim.

We talked for a bit longer, and something in Maxwell's comments hinted to something big coming up in the case. He continued on, but the impression remained with me.

"So, what are you up to this fall?" he asked.

"Well, I'm going to be heading up a juniors program at our Commonwealth School this fall."

Bobrowski looked at Maxwell. "Oh, really? When is that going to start?" he asked me.

"September."

This time, the glance between the two police officers was unmistakable. We finished our lunch, and Kirk and I left, but we both took with us a sense that something was finally going to happen.

The next thing we heard was that a big search was planned for Ely, Nevada. But unlike every other search that had happened to this point, the police were actually putting in calls to the media, alerting them, even *inviting* them to be part of it. I'd never seen them make such a big deal about a search until this point. We didn't know what evidence they had, but it was obvious that the police had big plans for the search.

They had other plans as well. They anonymously sponsored a Honk and Wave event to be held simultaneously in Washington and in Utah. They even provided the banners and got permission for the locations. Chuck headed up the one in Washington. Kiirsi, her girls, and my daughter Kristen participated in the one here in Utah.

We all waited anxiously to see what would be found. With this much attention, it was expected that they'd find a key piece of evidence, maybe even Susan's body. But the search was apparently fruitless. It was another trough in the roller coaster ride of emotions that we were always on.

On Saturday afternoon, the Honk and Wave commenced. Kiirsi described what it was like.

> *"Volunteers braved wind, rain, scorching heat, and sunburn to hold signs, smile, and wave at thousands of people who drove by, honked, gave thumbs up, and shouted things like, 'We hope you find her!' and, 'Our prayers are with you!'"*

But the event in Puyallup, Washington wasn't so rosy.

Perhaps coincidentally, the police had picked the corner directly across the street from the bank my dad visited every Saturday. Chuck and Judy and the other volunteers held their banners and waved at the passersby, and things seemed to be going well until my dad arrived on the scene.

My dad claimed that Chuck was spreading lies about Josh, and that the only goal of the event was to disrupt their lives.

"How is your standing on the corner of our neighborhood store helping to find Susan?" he asked, getting in Chuck's face.

Chuck reminded him of the restraining order that had been issued, but it didn't faze my dad. The news crews that were filming the Honk and Wave captured the conflict as it happened. The two fathers continued to argue until Josh pulled up with the boys in the car.

Cameras captured Josh's tortured, tear-stained face. "Chuck Cox uses my children as pawns in the media to drive whatever point he has," Josh stated.

When I saw the news story that night, I had to laugh at that last part. Here Josh was, driving over to the cameras with his boys in tow and claiming that it was Chuck who used them as pawns? His hypocrisy was astonishing.

Hot on the heels of that interchange came another big revelation. A friend of my dad's, a woman he had formerly dated, went public with the fact that he was obsessed with Susan.

She had reported the information to the police earlier, but now the story went through the media like a wildfire. She shared what it was like the couple of times they had dated.

"He was pretty open, often in a joking way, about having an interest in pornography," she said. Then she described another conversation.

She had asked him if he was involved with anyone. He laughed. "No. Susan is pretty much all I can think about." It wasn't the first time he had brought up his daughter-in-law. His friend thought he had some pretty serious hang-ups, and they fell out of touch.

This wasn't any surprise to those of us who were close to Susan. But the public was shocked by this disturbing revelation. My dad denied it outright, but the question had been raised, and now everyone wanted to know what Steve Powell had to do with Susan's disappearance.

Whether the police really did have evidence for Ely or not, whether they planned the interaction between Chuck and Steve, or the release of this new story, something that weekend seemed to make my dad and my brother relax a lot. Maybe they saw the fruitless search and assumed that there really was no evidence pointing at Josh. Maybe not. But they certainly opened up after that.

The next week, on August 26, they were both interviewed by Good Morning America. My dad appeared confident, even cocky. When he was asked about his relationship with Susan, he responded with a claim that they had a sexual relationship.

> "Father-in-law / daughter-in-law flirting with each other, maybe some sexual touching or whatever. And—I enjoyed it, frankly. Susan was a joy to be around in so many ways, not just those ways. Susan was very sexual with me. She was very flirtatious. I mean, I'm her father-in-law, and she would do a lot of things that . . . she did it, I did it. We interacted in a lot of sexual ways."

This was a complete contradiction to what he'd said from the beginning. Even a couple of days earlier, he'd told reporters that any claims that he had hit on Susan were lies.

His new statement about their relationship was disturbing enough, but then he told the Good Morning America crew that he had Susan's teenage diaries, and that he planned to post them on his website.

It wasn't surprising to me that when Josh was interviewed, he looked horribly defeated. He still claimed to have no idea what had happened to Susan, along with all of the other lies, but his face was haggard. I could only imagine it was hard for him to realize just how twisted our dad really was. Though he said Susan was flirtatious, even *he* denied that she had ever returned my dad's feelings.

His discouragement was founded, too. That afternoon, police arrived at their home with a search warrant. In the hours that followed, authorities seized five computers and loaded boxes and garbage bags. Pierce County and West Valley City police officers were working together, and they hauled off their finds for analysis.

We all waited to see what would come of it. I couldn't help worrying about the boys, but I hoped that, whatever they found, it would lead to an arrest.

CHAPTER TWENTY

The phone rang at midnight on September 22, 2011. I shot up in bed, my heart pounding. Who would be calling at this hour? Unless—

I grabbed the phone. It was Chuck. Maybe this was it. "Hello?"

"Hi, sorry to call so late, but I thought you'd want to know. Your dad has been arrested." Not Josh?

"My dad?" I'd always expected he would be arrested, but *along* with Josh, not instead of him. Kirk looked over at me with questioning eyes, and I waved at him to be patient.

"It was for voyeurism and child pornography. The boys have been removed from the home."

My groggy brain fought to take it in. My stomach churned at the mention of the charges, but the other, glorious fact outshined that darkness.

"Kirk, the boys are out of that house!" I stage whispered. It was hard to keep my voice quiet, to not wake the kids.

Chuck went on to explain that the boys were in foster care until the court could sort things out. My mind was spinning. Were they frightened? Did they know what was happening? I ached for the fear and uncertainty they must be experiencing, yet I knew they were safe. That kind of emergency foster care meant that Josh wouldn't even know where to find them. He couldn't get to them now. And soon, they would be under their grandparents' protective care.

I tried to listen as Chuck described what he knew of the arrest, but inside, I was jumping up and down for joy. Kirk took over the call and relayed bits of information back to me.

"They found stuff in your dad's house—photos of girls. Chuck doesn't know the details. The actual charges are unrelated to Susan's disappearance."

That was a disappointment. But I couldn't let it keep me down for long. Surely, this would bring a break in the case. And regardless of what happened there, the boys were safe.

Chuck promised to keep us up to date with any developments, and we hung up. Sleep was elusive then. How *could* I sleep? It appeared that something real was going to happen after almost two years of waiting.

Over the next few days, we were on pins and needles, eager for any bit of new information. Though I usually avoided watching the news, I started combing through it, looking for details.

As the case unfolded, the child porn charges were dropped, and the focus became the voyeurism. My dad had allegedly been taking photos of his little next-door neighbors while they bathed and used the restroom—all through the blinds over his windows and theirs.

Every time I thought about that, my stomach would churn again. It was another stark reminder of how sick he was, how far he'd sunk.

Another detail came out then that stunned the world, though it didn't surprise me a bit. There were hundreds of pictures found of Susan in my dad's things. Many of them were of her in various states of undress, and they were obviously taken without her knowing. Others were close-ups of her buttocks, legs, or breasts. She was fully dressed in these pictures, and, again, it was clear she had no knowledge of his presence. It was physical evidence of his obsession with her.

How guilty this made him look! Of course, the investigators had been seeing the hints of this obsession for months. But now, the media got wind of it, and it started to bring up all sorts of questions. They were the same questions I'd asked myself from the beginning. How much of Susan's disappearance was just Josh? What did my dad have to do with it? I didn't know for sure, but that suspicion of his involvement had been there all along, and now others were asking the same questions.

In the meantime, all we could do was watch and wait to hear what was happening with the boys.

A couple days later as I was doing laundry, I caught myself humming happily. The sound was so foreign that it stopped me in my tracks. I put the laundry basket down and leaned against the wall. When was the last time I'd been happy enough to hum like that? I couldn't even remember. Had it really been since before Susan's disappearance? Suddenly, I realized what a burden had been lifted. Knowing the boys were out of that house had changed me. My shoulders were straighter. I was smiling. And humming. I closed my eyes and offered a silent prayer of gratitude.

"Thank you for getting the boys to safety."

I picked up the laundry basket and carried it upstairs. I felt fifty pounds lighter.

It was amazing what hope could do.

For the last year, I thought I'd been prepared for the boys to come to us. Now that I realized how close it was getting, I was more eager than ever. And yet, I was more at peace. We knew we could get the call any minute to tell us they were with the Coxes.

On Monday, September 26, the judge awarded temporary custody to Chuck and Judy. I floated through the rest of the day.

"I wish we could go see them," I told Kirk that night. "But I don't want to step on any toes. They've been waiting as long as we have."

"I'm sure we'll get to go soon." He rubbed my shoulders. "Let's just be patient."

I sighed. Patience. I guess God apparently wanted me to learn some. It seemed like waiting was all I did.

Luckily, the next day, we had our Commonwealth School, an academic group run by parents for our homeschooled youth. I was in charge of the group for the younger kids, and I had tons to do. It was good to lose myself in interacting with the energetic children. I tried to keep my attention focused on our activity, but part of me was in Washington with the boys and their grandparents, experiencing the reunion from eight-hundred-and-fifty miles away.

My phone was in my purse, so I had no idea that Kirk had tried to call me more than a dozen times.

One of the other ladies in the group got a call on her cell phone. She answered it, then laughed and held it out to me.

"Jen, it's Kirk. He's been trying to reach you."

My heart fluttered in excitement. This could be good news. "What's up?"

"I've been trying to get hold of you all afternoon. Chuck called. He said he wished we could be there when the boys arrived. He thought it would make the transition easier. I think he's a little nervous."

"So . . ."

"Yes, he'd like us to come up."

"Tonight?" An electric jolt shot through me. Could I actually see the boys tonight?

Kirk laughed. "Yep. I checked the flights out, and it looks like there's one leaving in two hours. Could we make it happen?"

"Um, yeah!" There was no way I was going to miss out on this opportunity. "I'm on my way."

The other moms understood and took over so I could get out of there. I gathered up our kids and headed home. I called Jes on the way. She was in town and had been staying with us but had left that afternoon to head farther north to visit her parents. I hated to ask her to come back when she'd only just left, but I couldn't think of any other solution.

She didn't balk in the slightest. "I can stay and watch the kids. You should go!"

"Are you sure?" I felt bad putting her out like that.

"Absolutely. I'll get packed up and be there as soon as I can. This is awesome, Jenny."

I had to agree. My cheeks were already starting to hurt from smiling so much.

It was a mad dash to get everything ready so fast. I threw clothes in a bag, barely pausing to see what I was putting together.

And my children were great. Having Jes come back was a treat, and they knew how much it meant to me.

"We'll all go up there soon," I promised them. "Maybe in a couple of months. Let's just give them some time to settle in." It was hard for them to wait to see their cousins, but they were learning patience, too.

Two hours later, we were in the air. I took a deep breath and calmed down enough to realize that we were actually on our way.

I leaned against Kirk's shoulder and sighed. "This hardly seems real," I said.

"I know. But it is." He put his arm around me and held me close.

As the time went by, I couldn't help but compare this flight to the last one I'd made to Washington. Then, I had been trembling and distraught with the nerves and fear of my coming confrontation. Now, I was filled with excitement, hardly able to sit still in my seat.

And yet, there were still some twinges of apprehension. I knew what kind of lies Josh and my dad were capable of. I had no idea how the boys would receive us. Would they hate us, or, even worse, would they fear us? The lies that had been published online by my family kept trying to worm their way back into my mind—that I had hated Josh for years, that I had "stolen" property from his house (the personal items Chuck had asked me for), and so on. How much of that had the boys been subjected to? As the plane descended to the SeaTac airport, I firmly shoved aside my worries. We would weather whatever we needed to. We were in this for the long haul, after all.

Chuck and his sister, Pam, picked us up at the airport, and we started the nearly hour-long drive back to their house. I noticed immediately how nervous he was. He was fidgety and anxious.

What a change this all must be for them. They had been just as shut out as we had, only Chuck had been much closer physically to my dad. There had been plenty of bad blood between them. He was probably having the same fears that I was. My discomfort diminished in the face of his nerves. I could be a buffer between them. That was something I could contribute.

When we walked into the house, Braden was at the top of the stairs. I stopped inside the door and stared at him, taking in the changes that had come with eighteen months. He stared back, and I could see him measuring me for a second. But then a smile burst across his face, and he skipped down the stairs and flew into my arms. I caught him up and spun him around, squeezing him as tight as I dared.

"I love you," he said, his little voice close to my ear. Tears sprang to my eyes, and I swallowed to keep my voice even.

"I love you, too, Braden. I missed you."

Charlie came in from the living room, and I hugged him to my side. Kirk grabbed them and repeated the action. Their giggles and smiles were like water on dry, cracked ground. They soothed and filled the torn-up places in my heart.

With the greeting, the tension in Chuck evaporated. He told me later that he and Judy had been unsure of how to interact with them. Was it okay to hug them? Would the boys pull back or feel overwhelmed? With our arrival, the ice was broken, and we all relaxed.

Braden was a bounding ball of energy. He flitted from one thing to the next, demanding that we read him this book or look at that toy. He was in and out of my lap, all over Kirk, and echoed that with Chuck and Judy.

Charlie was more reserved at first. He sat close, but not touching, and he had a hard time verbalizing anything. I watched as he tried to tell me about a toy that Judy had. He had to think to form each distinct word, and it seemed awkward as he put them together. It was subtle enough that I wondered if I was really even seeing the issue, but Kirk noticed it, too.

I continued to try to draw him into conversation, and we all kept playing with Braden. Out of the corner of my eye, I could see Charlie inching closer. I kept my voice normal and my attention on Braden. Charlie appeared more comfortable that way.

I wanted to weep for the changes that had taken place in this innocent child. He had been through so much!

156

A few minutes later, Charlie got up and picked up a book from the stack Braden had made on the floor. He held it to his chest and looked at Kirk, then me. *Come on,* I thought. *Trust me. I won't let you down.* I looked up at him and caught his eye, then held out my hands.

A burst of joy washed over me as he took one step forward, then another, then climbed into my lap and snuggled in for story time.

The rest of the night sped by in a jumble of active boys and tired but happy adults. The boys didn't want to go to bed. After all, they'd only been there for a couple of hours, and I could see that their grandparents were reluctant to be firm with them. I understood their feelings, but as the boys got more and more wound up, I finally decided to step in.

"Okay, guys. It's time for bed. Let's get you changed and get your teeth brushed." There were groans and whines, but they obeyed. It was after ten thirty before they settled in.

I stood in the doorway, drinking in the sight of their peaceful faces. Every pain and worry for almost two years had led up to this moment. Kirk came to stand beside me, looking into the room over my shoulder. We didn't say anything. No words were needed.

Back in the living room, I sank into the couch with a sigh. It had been a long, crazy day.

"Thanks for coming," Judy said.

I shook my head. "No, thanks to *you* for inviting us. I hope we're not intruding too much on your time with them."

"It's been good. I think we would have tiptoed around each other much longer. I just didn't want to scare them away." She looked tired, but a smile still lingered. Her eyes brimmed with love for her grandsons.

Chuck laughed softly without humor. "You should have heard Charlie when he first got here. He wanted to know if we were going to start abusing him. I can only guess what has been said by . . . actually, let's not talk about that any more tonight. I'm exhausted, and I think Judy is, too." Judy nodded. Chuck got to his feet and held his hand out to her.

157

Jennifer Graves and E. G. Clawson

After they went to bed and Kirk and I settled in for the night, I lay awake for a while, soaking in the knowledge that the boys were truly in the next room—happy, safe, and surrounded by people who loved them.

I felt that Susan must be watching this night with joy. I fell asleep with her smile in my mind and peace in my heart.

CHAPTER TWENTY-ONE

For two-and-a-half blissful days, we played with the boys. We did crafts and read stories and cooked meals. Chuck and Judy had a lot of errands as they scrambled to have the necessities ready for caring for two small children. Car seats and groceries and all the accoutrements of childhood had to be bought. We consulted on the best brands and watched the boys so they could get the shopping done.

Kirk and I accompanied Chuck to a hearing, and we cheered silently along with him when the judge made their temporary custody official. Sitting in that little courtroom, I could picture what it would be like when we got the official ruling that they were with us to stay.

But as our visit went on, I noticed that they were talking a lot more about the boys being there long term. It had cropped up from time to time over the last month or so, but I hadn't really known how serious they were.

Part of me was extremely jealous. I had planned and hoped and prayed for their safe addition to our family for so long that it almost felt like Chuck and Judy were talking about taking away my own children. And yet, the more rational part of me knew that they were the grandparents and they loved the boys as much as I did.

"It'll break my heart," I whispered to Kirk as we lay in bed our last night there. "I can't imagine them never coming to live with us."

Kirk reached over and rubbed my arm. "I know."

I scooted over and tucked his arm around me. "You know what, though. It'll be okay. Everything is going to be okay now."

He didn't speak, just held me close. I took a deep breath. It would be hard to be the distant aunt, but I could do it if that was what needed to happen. I could see them on holidays and send them birthday presents in the mail. As long as they were away from my dad and my brother—that was all that mattered.

Besides, there was time to work this all out. No matter where Charlie and Braden lived, they were in our lives again.

The late September sunlight streamed through the kitchen windows, warming the kitchen. I hummed to myself as I peeled potatoes for dinner. Our visit with the boys had been so refreshing, yet I was happy to be home. There had been a sense of normalcy missing from our lives for so long. Just a touch of that was returning, and it felt like a long breath after being under water.

Kirk came upstairs and sat down at the counter.

"I just had an interesting conversation with your mom."

My good mood vanished immediately at his tone. "What did she say?"

"Well, it was hard to get anything specific out of her, but she basically said she wants to go to Washington and take care of your siblings."

Of course she did. I tossed the potato I was holding into the sink and leaned on the counter. "Did they ask her to come?"

Kirk shook his head. "I really don't know. I asked her the same question, but she hemmed and hawed around it so much . . . you know what it's like."

Yes, I did. Trying to talk to Mom about anything to do with Josh was an exercise in futility. It had been a year and a half, and she was still stuck in denial, sure that Josh had nothing to do with Susan's disappearance. And she knew exactly where I stood. Our conversations had degenerated to basic discussions over mealtimes, schedules, and the weather. We couldn't discuss Josh with any degree of civility anymore. What's more, Mom was reluctant to give us a straight answer about her contact with the rest of the family. I guess she knew that we would report anything to the police.

At least she still talked to Kirk sometimes.

We let the subject drop, but it nagged at me for days. And it didn't end there, either. Every day or two, she brought up the idea with Kirk. She didn't say the words, but 'poor Josh' seemed to radiate from her face. She did mention the fact that Alina and John had no one to take care of them. I understood her concern about John. His mental illness left him able to take care of his basic physical needs but not really able to live alone. But Alina and Josh were both adults. What did she think she could do?

And why was she supporting Josh?

Whenever Mom and I were in the same room, her unspoken worries were a silent buzz in my brain. Josh was alone. Josh was defeated and sad. Alina was worried. John was distraught. They all needed her.

Maybe that was it. They needed her. In hindsight, I can see how attractive that was to her after being shoved aside for so many years. But these were the people that had completely shunned me out, had blasted me in the news and online. It was more than hard to be sympathetic. At that moment, it was virtually impossible.

And Josh had killed Susan. I wanted to grab her by the shoulders and shake her. *Hello? He is a murderer!*

As far as I could tell, the only thing that kept her from running to Washington was her lack of money. She couldn't afford the travel and living expenses.

Her apprehensive expression nagged at me constantly. When was the last time she had put this much thought or worry into *my* family, *my* well-being? Part of me understood that I had the support, the great husband, the good friends, the solid life. But did that mean she should just walk away? Just stop caring about me the way a mom should care for her daughter?

After a particularly trying day, Kirk pulled me into the bedroom to talk. I thought he was going to commiserate with me.

"Why don't we encourage her to go?"

My jaw dropped. "What? Why should we send her up there to help 'poor Josh'?" I crossed my arms and sank down onto the bed. Was I the only one who saw how twisted this was?

"Well, think about it. Maybe she could be a good influence on him. She could try to talk him into a confession. I mean, your dad is gone now. And we've all seen what kind of influence he has over the rest of your siblings. Maybe with him gone . . ."

". . . maybe she can get them to see reality," I finished for him. "I hadn't thought about it that way."

"Remember what Josh was like when he was living with her after high school?"

I thought about the changes that had come over him during that time. He'd really pulled his life together then. He had gone to church and got a good job and stopped acting so much like my dad. Maybe . . .

"Do you truly think she could influence him?"

"I don't know. But it's worth a try, isn't it?"

A little flash of hope flared inside me. If she could convince Josh to do the right thing, to confess, maybe this whole nightmare could come to an end once and for all.

In the end, we decided to help her get to Washington for a visit. We gave her five hundred dollars and helped her make travel plans. Then we sent her off, our fingers crossed that she could inject some sanity and accountability into the situation.

When she called me a couple of days later, I hoped to hear some kind of progress being made.

"How are things going?" I asked. *Did you get him to talk?* I tried to keep my voice level.

"They're good. We had a great dinner tonight. I made spaghetti, and then we watched some TV. It was a pretty calm evening." She went on to describe the day-to-day activities—all of it very normal and on the surface.

I listened and made small talk. When we hung up, the frustration came slamming home.

From then on, it was clear that she wasn't going to have any positive influence over Josh. Her phone calls were glossy advertisements of the supportive mother. She didn't share anything of substance.

I tried to shrug it off. The boys were with their grandparents, my mom wasn't there to constantly bring up 'poor Josh,' and my dad was in jail. I had to just let things happen.

And beyond that, I was simply too tired of being on the verge of collapse all the time. I needed to feel happy. I concentrated on my family and our upcoming visit to the boys we were planning for Thanksgiving.

We were going to visit my aunt Lori, who had moved back to Washington, and spend some time with the Coxes and my nephews. My children couldn't stop talking about the upcoming trip, and the atmosphere in our home changed to one of cheerful anticipation. At last, there was something to look forward to.

The plans went along smoothly, and I found myself focusing more and more on our schooling and preparation for the holidays. I deliberately forced the frustrations with my mom out of mind whenever they came up. Mom was due back from her trip to Washington any day. I would deal with the situation when it arrived.

Then Chuck called one day.

I was sitting at the kitchen table working on math with Jason. He grinned impishly and scooted off the moment I answered the phone. I had to smile at his opportunism.

"Hi, how are things going with the boys?" I asked, turning my attention to the phone call.

"Oh, pretty good. They can be a bit of handful, of course, but that's just boys. Charlie's talking a lot more. All in all, I think they're doing well."

"I'm so glad. I can't wait to see you all next week."

"We're looking forward to it, too." We chatted a bit about boys and our plans, but I could tell that something was bothering Chuck.

"So, what else is going on? Is something the matter?" There were so many possible problems and worries being held at bay. I tapped the table with my pen, feeling suddenly jittery.

"Well, your mom has come by a couple of times to visit the boys."

"That's good, I guess. Did she say anything about Josh?"

Chuck was quiet for a second. "Hasn't she talked to you?"

Something in his voice sent more warning bells off in my mind. I cleared my throat. "She doesn't really tell me much about . . . well, about anything important."

"It seems like she's been helping Josh. She talked him into getting his own place. It looks like he's going to fight to get the boys back."

A wave of nausea rolled over me. I dropped my pen and leaned back in the chair. I probably shouldn't have been surprised.

"Is that so?" My tone was flat. This was *so* not what we had hoped for.

"That's not all." Chuck hesitated, as if what he had to say could top that news. "Apparently, she's also written an affidavit in support of Josh as a dad."

My jaw dropped. All my air seemed to be gone. *No. She wouldn't have done that. She couldn't really have gone that far, could she?* I took a deep, calming breath. "Are you sure?"

"I read it." His voice was hard, bitter.

Hot fury boiled up in my stomach. "What did it say?" I ground out.

"She called him a good, loving father." He paused and cleared his throat. "I'm not allowing her back in this home."

I couldn't believe it. She had never helped us in the case against Josh, and I knew she felt sorry for him. But she couldn't really have tried to support him after what he'd done.

Chuck was talking, but I couldn't listen. I had never felt so betrayed in all my life. She knew what he was. She knew what he had done. And she knew that I had spent the last couple of years doing anything and everything I could to make sure Charlie and Braden were safe.

"How could she?" My voice was barely a whisper.

I don't know how I ended the call with Chuck or how I told Kirk about what my mom had done. I only know that when she got home, later that same night, I wanted her gone.

How could I allow her back in my house when she was on his side?

"She can't live here anymore," I told Kirk as we had yet another heart-to-heart behind closed doors. "She has to move out. I can't *stand* that she did that!" My voice was rising along with the fury that had bubbled inside of me all day. Kirk could see that I was close to losing it.

"Let me go downstairs and talk to her. Maybe it's a misunderstanding." He hugged me and then walked out into the hall. I could see from his clenched jaw that her innocence in this case was a long shot.

They talked. I waited, anger and hurt and more anger boiling inside of me. When he came back upstairs, I could tell in an instant that it was true.

"She admitted it. She doesn't get what the problem is. She thinks that she was just doing what any loving, supportive mother would do for her son."

And there it was: the continuing denial that Josh had done anything wrong.

We let it rest that night, but we tried several times over the next few days to get through to her. No matter what we said, she simply didn't believe that she had done anything wrong. She saw her other children as victims in a horrible situation. She even said she thought my dad had gotten better over the years and that she was shocked when he was arrested. That was the last straw.

"Why can't you see it anymore, Mom? You lived with that man and finally found the courage to leave. You know better than anyone what he's like. You're the one who helped me see clearly. Why is it that I can see clearly now, but you can't?"

But it didn't matter. Nothing changed her mind.

In the end, we asked her to move out. We didn't boot her to the curb, but we told her she needed to start looking for another place to live.

Needless to say, our vacation to Washington was a badly needed break. We drove for thirteen hours, and the kids, loud and raucous in the car, were like a carnival of family fun around me. I soaked in the normalcy, the chaotic jumble of life. It was these little moments that kept me sane.

We stayed with Aunt Lori. She lived about forty-five minutes away from the Coxes. We didn't know what was planned for the actual holiday, but we were hoping we'd be able to spend it with the boys.

Before going out to dinner, we went to the Coxes' house to visit for a bit. My kids played and wrestled with the boys as I leaned against Kirk's shoulder. He looked down at me and smiled. I grinned back. This was so *good.*

"We'd love to have your family over for Thanksgiving dinner tomorrow," Judy offered. I did a little mental dance of happiness.

"That would be great."

"I don't know if you would like the idea, but we thought maybe you could take the boys home with you tonight for a sleepover. That way, I can finish up the baking."

The kids all heard that and perked up, freezing at their play. I could see the wheels turning: *what will Mom say?*

"What do you think, Kirk? Have they been good enough to have a sleepover?"

Kirk looked around, pretending to consider the idea. "Hm, that's a tough question. Well, I guess."

There were shouts and cheers from all the kids, and I laughed. Even fifteen-year-old Jeffrey was excited about the idea.

We all went out to a buffet restaurant that evening. Charlie and Braden were thrilled to be with their cousins, and the energy and excitement had them both wound a little too tight.

Braden wanted to eat nothing but dessert. Judy was obviously feeling frazzled by constantly chasing after these high-energy boys.

"They don't like vegetables," she said, almost apologetically.

"I totally understand. Things are different now than when they were staying with their dad."

Judy leaned in and lowered her voice. "That's true. We've been having a hard time getting them to wear pajamas at night. Charlie says they always slept nude with Josh."

We both shuddered, not knowing what other details might come out.

But this was supposed to be a happy occasion. I fixed my smile back in place and patted her hand. "Let me help out." I stepped in, hoping to give her a bit of a break.

"Braden, you have to eat a vegetable and some chicken before you have ice cream. Do you want to pick the food?"

He pouted for a minute, but when I didn't capitulate, he nodded. I took him to the counter and helped him dish up a few choices.

The rest of the evening was a jumble of food, car seats, sleeping bags, and late-night giggling. We finally got everyone settled in on Lori's living room floor. I looked out over the crowd of sleeping forms, from Jeffrey on down to Abigail, at seven, then Charlie and Braden at six and four. They seemed to flow, my children and Susan's children blending together into one big family.

The next day was a wonderful holiday. We ate and laughed and napped and enjoyed all the traditional Thanksgiving-ness.

"You know, this has been a really great few days," Chuck said as the adults lingered around the table. The kids had gone in the other room to watch TV, and it was finally quiet.

I smiled. "For us, too. We were worried about intruding on your holiday."

"No. It's been good." He lowered his voice. "We had started to wonder if we should keep the boys with us permanently. But." He glanced over at Judy. "Honestly, they're wearing us out. We want to be in their lives, but I just don't think it's right for us to be their full-time parents. They are such a natural fit with you."

Tears sprang to my eyes. My voice was thick with emotion. "It feels that way for us, too."

"I think that at least by the summer, things should be wrapped up, legally. We were thinking that we could take the boys to Disneyland. You know, something fun with Grandma and Grandpa. Then we'll bring them to you."

I looked at Kirk and he smiled. "That sounds perfect," he said.

When we left a couple of days later, it wasn't hard to say goodbye. Only a little while longer and they would be with us permanently.

CHAPTER TWENTY-TWO

N ow it was back to the waiting game. The rest of this story would be played out in the courts, we knew, and we anxiously watched for any further developments.

Josh had rented a house and was working to try to get the boys back. We were kept up to date on each miniature development by the constant calls, texts, and emails from reporters. Most of the time, I got my news in a Jeopardy-style fashion.

What do you think about the fact that the police found hundreds of pornographic images on your brother's computer? I read the email and snorted in disgust.

"Kirk, look at this. Apparently, Josh's computer has all kinds of garbage on it." He came over and read the email over my shoulder.

"That's not a shock."

Sometimes I'd respond and tell them I hadn't heard about it before. Sometimes I ignored it. The constant buzzing of my phone and knocking on my door had just become background noise over the last two years.

Christmas passed happily. I sent gifts to the boys and talked to them on the phone, but mostly it was just a nice, quiet holiday at home. As 2012 was ushered in, I couldn't help a thrill of excitement. This was the year that things would be resolved at long last.

What do you expect to happen at this next hearing? The text message asked the same question I was asking myself. It had been almost exactly six months since the boys had been taken from Josh. He had one weekly visit supervised by a caseworker. At first, that was it for his visits, but then a local pastor, trying to help Josh, offered to arrange another visitation opportunity. This next hearing would be reevaluating his case. Should he regain custody, or should the boys stay with their grandparents? I couldn't imagine that the judge wouldn't be able to see the improvement in the boys, but I was nervous just the same.

I didn't go to the hearing, but I anxiously waited for Chuck to call afterward.

The reporters beat him to it.

What do you think will be revealed by the polygraph test?

I stared at the text message, my stomach flipping over. Polygraph?

The phone rang and I jumped. It was Chuck.

"Hello?" My heart was pounding.

"It was amazing," he said without preamble. "This is it."

"Wait, tell me exactly what happened." I sank down onto the living room couch and leaned back. *Please, let this be it.*

"The police testified that the pornographic images on Josh's computer were cartoons depicting incestuous acts between parents and children."

A sick anger bubbled up into the excitement.

"But . . . that's horrible."

"There's more. The judge told Josh that he doesn't get the boys back yet, and he has to undergo a psycho-sexual evaluation." He paused, but I could tell there was more. "And he has to take a polygraph test."

I closed my eyes and took a breath. "A polygraph? This *is* it," I whispered, echoing Chuck's earlier words.

"Yep."

All of my hopes for this year were laid out perfectly before me. With a polygraph, they would be able to ask him anything. He had run out of time.

I floated through the rest of the day after talking to Chuck. My phone buzzed constantly, but I ignored most of it, agreeing to only one phone interview.

Inside, I was happy but also mentally holding my breath. This last, delicate piece of the puzzle needed to be placed, and I would breathe comfortably once it was done.

◆ ◆ ◆

Four days later, we had all settled into our comfortable after-church Sunday routine. The kids were downstairs reading, watching movies, and playing with toys. Kirk was in his office catching up on emails, and I had snuggled into bed with a book.

The phone rang, and I picked it up to see Kiirsi's number. She probably wanted to chat about the ruling again. We'd all been so excited.

"Hello," I said cheerfully.

She was sobbing. "Jenny, there was an explosion and . . . a reporter called me. He said that they're all dead. I tried to call Chuck. I can't even . . ."

Sick dread poured over me, and I sat up. "Slow down, Kiirsi. What happened?"

"I can't . . . the house exploded." She couldn't get a sentence completed between the sobs. My heart felt like it was being squeezed, and I realized I was holding my breath. I drew in a ragged gasp.

If Kiirsi was this upset, I knew it had to be about the boys. "Have you talked to Chuck?" I asked.

"I couldn't." She was hysterical, and I had to get off the phone. I needed information. Now.

"Kiirsi. I'll call him and call you back. Calm down, okay."

She mumbled something and hung up. I sat still for one second and then threw back the covers and got out of bed.

Stay calm, I told myself. Breathe.

I walked across the hall to Kirk's office and closed the door behind me.

"What's up?" he said absently as I grabbed his shoulder. Then he caught a glimpse of my face. He stood up and reached out for

171

me, supporting me by my arms. "What's the matter?" His voice had a new edge.

I fought to keep my voice steady. "Kiirsi said something about an explosion and that 'they're all dead' and I have to call Chuck." I took several long, deep breaths, but the walls were closing in around me. I tried to dial Chuck's number, but my hands were shaking so hard that it took forever.

When he answered, I forced myself to be strong. I could hear he was driving.

"Chuck, what's going on?" I knew the edge of panic was creeping into my voice.

"We don't know for sure. I'm almost there. I'll call you back in ten minutes."

I hung up, and the shaking started to spread until I was trembling all over. Kirk pulled his chair over, and I fell into it.

One minute passed. Then another. Kirk got online and started looking for any shred of news. There were tweets and facebook comments about a fire, but no one knew anything yet.

Three minutes turned into ten minutes, then fifteen. My shaking turned to quiet crying, then sobs. I kept seeing Braden at the top of the Coxes' stairs when we had visited that first time. His grin and then his laughter as he launched himself into my arms. *Oh, dear God, please don't let this be true.* I uttered the prayer over and over again.

Kirk picked up his phone and called Chuck back. I watched as his face turned to a mask of anguish.

"No!" I wailed. I crumpled into a ball on the floor, and Kirk wrapped one arm around me while trying to still get details from Chuck. How was this even possible? How could these little boys have gone through so much and be so close to getting free and then die in a fire?

But the details were worse than that. Josh had killed them. He had locked the caseworker out of the house and blown himself and the boys up.

He'd struck again.

We stayed in the office with the door closed. I couldn't make myself move from that spot. I don't know how much time passed, but I knew I needed to tell people. I called Kiirsi back and told her what Chuck had said, but a reporter had already beaten me to it. My Aunt Lori, my cousin Jessica, Debbie Caldwell, other friends and family—they all needed to know.

I held my phone and stared at it through my tear-blurred eyes, trying to decipher the foreign-looking symbols. Oh, wait, they were just letters. How did this thing work again? It took forever to compose a text that would convey all the information.

In the end, it was something like, *Josh just blew up his house and the boys were with him and they're all dead.* Later, I felt so bad for the people who heard it from me. What a horrible way to find out. Of course, there was no good way to hear that kind of news, but when I later heard how some of them had found out, it broke my heart.

Jes was in church when she got the message. She was in the middle of Relief Society, a class for women. She felt her phone buzz and she read the message and then just stood up in the middle of the room. The teacher and all the rest of the women turned to look at her, expecting her to say something. She stood there for a minute, frozen in place. Then she walked out of the room, got her husband and son, and left the building, not a word to anyone.

Chuck had been in a church planning meeting. Church hadn't started yet, and Judy was still at home. One of his friends had seen something on Facebook and called him on his cell phone. Chuck's bishop offered to drive him to Josh's house to see if it was true. Not wanting to worry Judy until he knew the details, Chuck didn't call her right away. A few minutes later, she showed up at church and was confused by the stares and whispers that swirled around her when she walked in. A well-meaning friend pulled her aside.

"Why are you here?"

Judy was confused. Why shouldn't she be at church? Her friend had to break the news.

She and Marie, Susan's youngest sister, went home to wait for the news. Their ward only held one of their three meetings, then cancelled the rest and sent everyone home. Everyone who heard the news, whether they were friends, family, or even strangers, was devastated.

And I huddled in the corner of Kirk's office and sobbed.

Kirk called my mom, who was staying with my uncle. I couldn't talk to her. The only thing I could think was that I was glad she wasn't here.

"Mom, Brother and Sister Crowther are at the door for you," Kristen called through the office door.

The Crowthers were our neighbors across the street. The news was out for sure. I scrubbed my sleeve across my face and cleared my throat.

"I'll be right down." I hoped my voice was somewhat normal.

As I walked down the stairs, I saw Tawni Crowther standing in the living room. Her eyes were filled with concern.

"You've heard," I said, then looked at my kids standing there. "You don't know yet," I whispered, my voice cracking. I stumbled down the last few stairs and called them around me. Kirk came down behind me.

"Kids, Charlie and Braden are dead. Josh killed them in a fire." I winced, hearing the harshness of my words, but then I straightened my spine. My children knew what Josh was. I hadn't been able to protect them from that. Tawni knelt down and put her arm around Abigail, and we all hugged and cried together.

The day was a blur. With something that big, the reporters don't call and text. They just show up. Our front yard became a media circus, and we were trapped inside yet again. My loving neighbors were brave enough to muscle through and come to our aid.

I huddled in the rocking chair in the living room and cried. My friend, Shauna Simpson, came over and sat on the floor next to me. She held my hand and listened to me as I babbled incoherently.

Finally, Shauna asked the kids if they wanted to come to her house. They were all sad, but, as kids usually do, they needed distractions. I was useless. It was the dearest kindness that she showed in helping my children through that dark time. All of them wanted to go but Jeffrey. He was worried about me. Kirk was trying to deal with the media, and Jeffrey didn't want to desert us.

Our other friends, the Platts, came by, too. They brought dinner, and Dave Platt could tell that Jeffrey was overwhelmed. He talked Jeffrey into going to their house. I was so grateful. I knew Jeffrey hated to see me cry. He kept coming over to hug me and kiss me, trying to make me feel better. But hugs and kisses couldn't help me. At that moment, nothing could.

The reporters were getting pushier, and Kirk went outside to answer questions. He didn't have a coat on, and they kept him out in the cold forever. Later, I watched the news piece, and, as always, I was awed by how graceful he was in handling the horror.

As the day went on and the reporters dwindled, I went outside to be with Kirk. He spoke to the media, the few who were left at this late hour, while I sat on the step behind him. One photographer asked if he could come in and capture what this was like for us. I don't know why, but I let him in. He hung around quietly and took pictures and made a few notes. It was bizarre. But nothing could intrude on my pain.

The boys are dead.

That sentence kept running through my mind until it had changed and morphed into a foreign language. And yet, the agony of that truth couldn't be changed. It was a razor slashing across my heart.

So what do you do? How do you go on? I don't know how we got through that day, but we did. We cried and talked and sat silently and leaned on friends and held each other. We even ate meals and drank water and all of the things that sustain life. The day was an eternity and an instant.

And the next day dawned. That's when the reality really hit. There was no more custody battle, there was no more hoping and planning for our family's new additions. There was no more hope that Josh would confess to Susan's murder. It was all over.

The details came out over the next days—the hatchet Josh had used to chop their small bodies, the bungled 911 call, the plans Josh had made, and his final messages to some of my siblings—it was sickening and numbing at the same time.

Yet the more I thought about it, the more little morsels of peace began to creep into my heart.

Josh had obviously felt trapped by the ruling at his last hearing. In his desperation to keep the boys to himself, he had actually freed them from his grip. If I believed in Heaven—and, oh, how I did—then I knew in my soul that Susan and her boys had been reunited.

Josh had done everything he could to keep them apart, but he had failed. Completely. Susan had won the custody battle—forever.

And he had proclaimed himself forever and without a doubt to be a murderer. It brought a grim sort of justice to the situation. *Nothing* could make it okay that he had harmed his sweet, innocent sons. *Nothing* could make that okay. But, he couldn't hurt them anymore. And everyone now knew what he was.

CHAPTER TWENTY-THREE

A year and a week after the boys were killed, my brother, Michael, took his own life by jumping off a seven-story parking structure. He had moved to Minnesota not quite a year after Susan had disappeared, but I knew the local police still had him in their sights. Presumably, he had some piece of information that would help shed light on the case.

It was one more wound, tearing at my heart.

According to my mom, there was absolutely no reason for Michael to commit suicide. He was just fine. She still has no idea where his desperation came from.

I could only shake my head again. It was guilt. The police knew Michael had information—at least, they had hinted strongly in that direction in our conversations. Josh must have told him his secrets, and Michael had finally decided he couldn't live with the burden anymore.

To me, as heartbreaking as it was, it made some sort of sick sense. Every one of my brothers had been deeply influenced by my dad. Josh was a murderer. John was wracked by mental illness. And now Michael was also gone.

But I had no idea how right, or how wrong, I was.

Months later, as the time for my dad's release from prison drew near, Detective Maxwell called.

"I wanted you to know that we have a couple more things to wrap up in the next week or two, and then we'll be releasing everything to the public. There's just no one else to pursue."

I was shocked. "What about my dad?"

"There just wasn't any hard evidence that he was involved. Maybe he overheard Josh and Michael talking . . . but his alibis all check out."

I was confused. "Michael? So there was evidence of him being involved?"

Detective Maxwell paused for a moment before answering. "There was a lot of circumstantial evidence to tie Michael to Susan's disappearance. Honestly, we think word may have gotten back to him about a specific search we made of a property. We thought her body might be there. That was only a couple of days before he killed himself."

I was silent, trying to take it in. Maxwell continued. "I just wanted you to have a heads-up about the release of information."

Everything was going to be released—the story about me wearing a wire to my dad's house when I confronted Josh, everything.

Kirk talked to Chuck the next night, and more details came out about Michael. There was strong evidence that suggested Michael was the one to meet Josh halfway when Josh had been putting all those miles on the rental car. I'm still unclear on the time frame, but at some point, Michael's car broke down in a little town in Oregon, almost exactly four-hundred miles from Salt Lake City, and instead of taking it to be repaired or even selling it, he took it straight to a junkyard and asked for it to be demolished.

The police got to the car before it was destroyed. They brought in cadaver dogs, which immediately reacted to the car. Whatever they were smelling was located in the trunk, but there wasn't enough DNA evidence to point directly to Susan.

As Kirk relayed this information, I fought to draw a good breath. I wasn't sure which was more devastating—that there was so much evidence against Michael, or that there was nothing against my dad.

But the reality of my dad's involvement was still clear, to me if to no one else. Even if he didn't participate in Susan's actual death, he still actively drove a wedge between her and Josh for years. As much as anyone else who didn't physically pull the trigger or plunge the knife, he was a part of Susan's murder.

Over the next few days, I was haunted by a conversation I'd had with Kirk and Chuck shortly after the boys' funeral.

"The police are pursuing Michael for after-the-fact knowledge," Chuck said.

Kirk and I glanced at each other. "Well, I guess it's not a surprise," I said. "We've felt all along that they've been covering for him. It's a fortress over there."

Now I started to put that conversation together with another one I'd had with Michael when he'd first come home from Korea. He'd been honorably discharged from the army, and he came to stay with us for a couple of nights before going on to Washington.

"Hey, Jenny. Do you know that in Asia they have a deep sense of family honor?" He leaned back against the sofa cushions, and his eyes were distant, as if lost in memory. "They will do anything to maintain that honor. Even murder, suicide, or covering up a crime."

"That's a twisted sense of honor, if you ask me," I said. I wasn't sure what to make of that brief interchange, but it was now obvious that this "honor code" had left a big impression on him. Had he taken this belief to heart, not only covering for Josh's secrets, but creating some of his own?

And yet, it was Michael, my sweet little brother, who was now gone. I was heartbroken for the loss of both his life and his innocence. I remembered again that conversation between Josh and my dad all those years ago. "Mom thinks she can control Michael?" Josh had asked. "No, *we* control Michael."

That day in January 2010, when I had confronted Josh and my dad, Michael was standing right there, pulling Josh away from me and out the door. And I never thought to ask *him* where Susan's body was.

179

PART FOUR:

MOVING FORWARD

"There is not enough darkness in all the world to put
out the light of even one small candle."
-Robert Alden

CHAPTER TWENTY-FOUR

Somehow, we got through those first unimaginable days after the boys' deaths. The funeral came and went, and we realized that we had to face life as it was now.

For more than two years, my entire life had revolved around bringing Josh to justice and getting Susan's boys to safety. All of that was gone.

What had it all been for? Why had I felt such a driving need to do my part? What had been the purpose of all the anguish and fighting for the boys? I had all of those questions and more running through my head in a pounding rhythm that threatened to rip me to shreds.

So I started to write. I struggled with each word that I put on paper, but I had to get the story out of me so I could start to heal. I found Emily, and together we began to try to put the years of suffering into order, to tell my story.

And something started to change. The sick grief inside of me was gradually, gradually accompanied by peace. It wasn't gone, and the pain was still ever present, but it was tempered with a realization that Susan and the boys didn't have to die in vain. Their story could help others get to safety. If law enforcement agencies were willing to look hard at the details, maybe they could eventually learn how to make much-needed adjustments.

And we could all look at them and see that we have a responsibility to break the chain of violence.

I was talking to a friend a while ago, and she asked me an interesting question. "Did your dad ever kidnap you guys, the way his parents kidnapped him?" She was referring to the so-called "kidnapping game" he had written about where his parents would steal him and his siblings from each other.

"No, he never did anything like that," I said. But for some reason, that question stayed with me. I kept mulling it over and over in my mind until a realization dawned. He didn't technically kidnap any of us, but he did manage to wrest all four of my siblings away from my mother. He twisted their minds until they could no longer see what truth or right was. In my opinion, that was worse than just physically removing them from their mother.

And then there was Josh. He kidnapped his boys in the ultimate way, by taking their very lives. The revelation astounded me, and I saw so clearly that not only does the cycle of violence continue from generation to generation, it often escalates.

Someone has to stop it.

Chainbreakers Foundation's motto is: "We cannot liberate victims. We can only educate them. They must liberate themselves."

That is why we wrote this book.

I look back at Susan's life and the choices she made. It breaks my heart again every time I realize she is gone. She was my friend, my sister. We spent our time together discussing ways to be better mothers and daughters of God. We had plans to raise our children together and dreams for the future. I still believe that one day, I will see her and the boys again, but, for now, those dreams are gone.

I can't judge her for not getting away from Josh, but I do regret it constantly. What more could I have done or said to help her? What if . . .

There are too many endings to that statement, and they will drive me insane if I dwell on them. All I can do is go forward and determine with every ounce of strength that I will *not* permit the cycle of my family to reach my children.

I have received emails and personal statements from women telling me they, or someone they know, have escaped their abusive marriages after hearing Susan's story. I have seen the compassion and love that has been poured out by friends and family and even total strangers. All of us see the tragedy that didn't have to happen.

And this is what I want to share with you who are suffering.

It is time to end the suffering for yourselves and for your families. Turn to your friends and family, to your church leaders or local shelters, and get out now. It may seem impossible, intensely frightening, but you can do it. You are not alone. Don't wait until it's too late.

The wonderful news is that on the other side of that scary step is a new life for you. A life that you can live without fear and without being stepped on. It's a life where you can raise your children in peace. Please do not let Susan's story become your own.

To you who are trying to end the cycle of abuse in your own families—it will be hard. Many of the people who should support you and stand by you will hate you. They will treat you like the enemy, just as my family has treated me. But you have to be brave and make the change, or this cycle will continue on to your children, your grandchildren, and so on.

I have been ostracized by my family, not only by my father and my siblings, but, to a lesser degree, by my mother's family as well. They blame me for asking my mother to move out. They think I abandoned her in her greatest time of need.

Immaculée Ilibagiza, a hero of mine, had to leave her beloved homeland, Rwanda, in order to heal. I knew that I needed that physical distance to heal the relationship with my mom. I have to accept that I can't make everyone happy. I can only set the boundaries that keep my children happy and safe, and *they* are my ultimate responsibility.

One year after the boys were murdered, Kiirsi put together a candlelight vigil to remember them and Susan. It was freezing cold and dark in the park. We were invited to gather together—Kiirsi, Debbie Caldwell, our family, and other friends. I was dreading it. I

185

wanted to remember Susan, Charlie, and Braden on their birthdays and on holidays, to think of them in the happy moments as they had been in life. This seemed to be another time to think only of the sadness of losing them.

But how would it look if I didn't go? I pulled myself together, bundled up my kids, and we headed to the park. As soon as I arrived, a sense of peace and comfort washed over me. The ever-present camera crews and news vans were there, bright lights blazing, but somehow it only added a glow of warmth to the otherwise frigid air.

As people arrived, they talked with hushed voices, offering hugs and comforting words. I looked around at the gathering crowd and was overcome by a deep sense of gratitude. These were the people who understood what it was like to have lost someone so dear. They were my companions in grief, and yet here they were, smiling and embracing and sharing their favorite memories.

As we lit candles and began the program, I knew I was in the right place.

Friends shared their thoughts, Alex Boye sang a beautiful arrangement of "I Can Only Imagine," and then a screen went up and the slideshow began.

The sweet strains of "Susan's Song: A Dream Away" began to play. The song had been written by my friend Camilyn Morrison and performed by Jessie Funk. It had been a treasure to me over the last few months. As the beautiful words and music played, pictures of Susan and her boys filled the screen and sent a glow of light across the faces of our friends.

Tears sprang to my eyes as I realized what a blessing Susan, Charlie, and Braden had been in my life. Of course, I missed them and would have given anything to have them alive and well again. But I had known them and loved them, and that was a gift in and of itself. My faith in God and in a life to come was strengthened even more as I watched the slideshow. There was such a feeling of love and companionship that it was overwhelming.

That night was a moment of closure for me. I know that we may never find Susan's body. We may never learn the details of the night she disappeared. But I can move on and know that at least

Susan and her boys have been reunited. That is light enough to keep the darkness at bay.

As Camilyn's lyrics say, "We long to see you. We long to hold you inside our arms again. But until then please don't cry, keep our memories alive. We'll be a dream away until the day we wake."

Susan. Charlie. Braden. I will stand as your witness and keep your memories alive until I see you again.

♦ ◆ ♦

For more details or help in breaking the chain
of domestic violence, please visit
www.ChainBreakerFoundation.com,
www.SusanCoxPowellFoundation.net
or seek help immediately at your
local shelter or police station.

You do not have to face this alone!

♦ ◆ ♦

ACKNOWLEDGEMENTS

Thank you to my Father in Heaven who inspired me to write this book – and then wouldn't let it leave my mind until I acted on it. He's blessed us in countless ways, comforted me and sent me good people to brighten my life when it seemed the darkness was winning.

Thank you to Kirk, my best friend and husband. You have encouraged and supported me as I've dedicated many many hours to writing this book. You've been my rock to lean on through the trials of the last few years. You have always been there to pick up the pieces when my heart was breaking yet again. I love you forever!

Thank you to Emily. You have patiently provided a listening ear and a shoulder to cry on as I've labored to move this story from my head and heart onto paper. Heavenly Father sent you to me because He knew I couldn't have done this project without you.

Thank you to Chuck and Judy Cox (Susan's parents). I wish the circumstances could have been a happier opportunity to get to know you. You welcomed us into your hearts and homes with the expectation of us raising your grandchildren. Despite that not being possible now, we still think of you as our adopted parents!

Thank you to our family who stood by us throughout this. It meant more to me than you can ever know.

Thank you to friends, new and old. Thank you to our neighborhood, ward, commonwealth, and homeschool communities, and the many many other people who have joined us on this journey. You have been extraordinarily loving and kind to me and my family. In person, through emails, Facebook, and so many other ways you've been supportive and encouraging. You were there for me and my family when the boys were murdered, to hold our hands, bring us meals, and care for our other children. We were able to travel to Washington for the boys' funeral because of the generosity of many. Your kind words have helped to keep me going through many tough times. Thank you!

Thank you, Mom, for being my first guiding light on this Earth.

ABOUT THE AUTHORS

Jennifer Graves is the mother of 5 beautiful children, 2 girls and 3 boys. She and her husband have been happily married for 19 years and together have been active in their community and church. Jennifer is the sister of Josh Powell who killed his 2 sons, Charlie and Braden, as well as himself in February of 2012, and is also believed to have killed his wife, Susan Cox Powell, in December of 2009.

She is the recipient of the 2013 ChainBreaker of the year Award, given for breaking the chain of abuse and violence in her family.

She enjoys homeschooling their children and mentoring in classes for the commonwealth school they attend. She also loves reading, playing card and board games, and learning new things. Most of all she loves to spend time with her husband and children. They currently reside in West Jordan, UT.

Emily Clawson is an author, a mother and a mentor. She traditionally writes inspirational fiction. This book has been a life changing experience for her and she is grateful to have been a part of telling this story. She resides in Taylorsville with her husband and four children where they run their leadership mentoring programs for youth. For details about her other books and updates about *A Light in Dark Places*, please visit www.emilygrayclawson.com.